Oct.

Dear Birke

Thank you
dear friends for
all the great years
of memories with
you. The high
school years of
times with Spenser
and his writings
for memories of
more great times.
How blessed
we are!

Love,
Karen &
Tom

Eating
LIFE® cereal
with a
bigger spoon
than most

Eating LIFE® cereal with a bigger spoon than most

By

Spenser J. Somers

Introduction By

&Carolyn Rebholz
Karen Somers

Copyright © 1997 Karen S. Somers and
        John O. Somers

"Graduation Address" and "Listening to Snow"
Copyright © 1990 Karen S. Somers and John O.
Somers

All Rights Reserved
First Edition

Library of Congress Catalogue Card Number:
        97-94154

ISBN 0-9659779-0-0

Published by Life's Destinations Co.,
P.O. Box 390018, Minneapolis, Minnesota
55439-0018.
612-943-1665

Design, composition and printing in the United
States of America by Bolger, Minneapolis,
Minnesota

Book Design – Jane Eschweiler

LIFE is a registered trademark of The Quaker
Oats Company and is used with permission.

Dedication

Sam   The wise man from the east.

Sage   The well-dressed angel who never wore a halo because it would mess up her hair.

Spenser   A shepherd who tends to sleep too much and his sheep lose direction.

Dad   A king with plenty of gold which he gives with extreme generosity.

Mom   The innkeeper who welcomes them all, her home never too full, except when she's redecorating.

They heard Christmas was being celebrated in the Somer-time, so they all headed to where they could find the greatest love beneath a tree.

Table of contents

Introduction

by Carolyn Rebholz

Spenser had an aura about his writing which was in tune with an ageless world. Through his writing he revealed his inner self and personal commitment to share all that mattered to him. He had a unique ability to hear, see, think, absorb, experience, and express himself in ways somehow different from other individuals his age. His quality of work created valuable insight into his personal vision of life and living. Spenser wrote prolifically on corners of envelopes, the proverbial napkin, a trunk full of notebooks and, of course, several journal books. Countless hours were needed to unleash and to translate his cryptic writing and terse phrases into order and form. Spenser's mother, Karen, and I were driven to achieve this goal of publishing his work and so became his literary management team. His precocious insight challenged us to enable others in the world to share it. To date hundreds, possibly thousands of people, young and old, have been moved by pieces of his work.

One of Spenser's splendid attributes of human nature was his endowment of unique perceptions. Some people hold these close, but a few are blessed with the knack to have the world as a potential audience. This was Spenser. In his captured thoughts, he saw the world at a slant: one of love, compassion, fun and frolic, and blatant truths that are commonly diluted by societal changes.

Spenser never worried that this writing would rupture his privacy or his personal life. He never worried about the effect his writing had on his intimate friends. He wrote from his soul with a foresight unknown to most of his peers. Writing with a sense of integrity and an emotional honesty, he appeals to everyone. His writing energy and spirit come through in his work with an urgency which makes his words timely and provocative.

No one can predict exactly who else among the present practitioners of the writing craft will represent this generation for the future. However, Spenser wrote volumes for himself and as these are shared, his presence will continue to move his readers.

I am honored to have been one of Spenser Somers' teachers, his friend, and the literary co-editor of the works he left behind. God bless all who are touched by his work.

Dearest Spenser,

I've never written a letter to you before. I've journaled as you taught me; I've prayed more as you taught me; I've talked to you at your place of rest at Lakewood Cemetery; I pray to you in your heavenly home; I've pleaded with you to come back; now I'm compelled to write to you. My tears stain the paper as I search for endearing words to express to you how my grief journey in losing you has lead me to uncovering and printing your soul-warming thoughts and enclosed writings.

Your Edina High School Creative Writing teacher said, "You had a gift of the 'Golden Pen.'" I knew you wrote many nights. Our family respected your privacy as you were immersed in creative pursuits; however, when I randomly found, through the years, your written words of wisdom, observations, images of peace, or messages of joy and nature, I stuck them away for safe keeping. The collection of papers was put in desk drawers, dresser drawers, under my bed, under your bed, in the downstairs bathroom cabinets — put away to enjoy at a later time. You were the unfinished artist, always wanting to improve your writing and your desire to be a writer. You shared with me many of your ideas and often read your writings to me. At times I didn't know how to respond to you because if I lavished too much praise, you would feel that as your pleased mother, I wasn't being objective. If I offered criticism, you would tell me I didn't really understand what thoughts or ideas you were expressing. So mostly, I kept things in my heart, cherished your presence, and kept your writings in safe places. When friends ask me, "How did you ever save all of these writings?" I don't really know. Perhaps I've known in the recesses of my mind that your written words would be your voice talking to me recapturing memories long after you were no longer going to walk through the front door.

In my deep loss for you and in my grief journey, I began "uncovering" your writings. I have sorted through myriad piles of paper. I separated literally thousands of cards and letters from friends, huge folders of medical information, your art work, newspaper articles, high school activities and photographs. Separately, I stacked your writings. Through the process I desperately missed not being able to share the mysteries of life, memories of the past and plans for the future with you.

Our family moved to Edina, Minnesota from the countryside in Ottawa, Kansas in the summer of 1984. Dad's job in Kansas City brought him here as legal counsel for Republic Telcom. Sage was a beautiful, happy second grader and Sam was an active ninth grade student at Valley View Junior High. You became an "all-star" baseball player, and were a leading player on the seventh grade traveling basketball team.

Then your world changed. In the summer of 1985 you found a "lump" while itching a mosquito bite on the right side of your lower abdominal area. On July 1, 1985 during a 4-1/2 hour surgery, your spleen and part of your stomach were removed along with a malignant cancer tumor that had developed and grown. Dad and I were at Minneapolis Children's Hospital's surgery waiting room as Dr. Stacy Robeck, your surgeon, shocked us with stunning diagnosis.

Dr. Larry Singher became your oncologist and trusted friend. Our world changed, too.

My dear Spenser, your life with us ended on November 9, 1990. This book, published entirely as you wrote it, is your amazing journey as a teenager, philosopher, and Christian.

So you see Spenser, my passion for you has driven me to spend my past few years of extra hours compiling your book. I have a great need to explain this process — not because of what I have done — but for you to know my motives.

Six months after our visits ended, I approached your very favorite creative writing teacher, Mrs. Carolyn Rebholz, and asked her if she would consider helping put your writings together. A few days later she came to our home to view the six-foot long, dark oak, antique bench pew dated 1798 filled with the entire writings of Spenser J. Somers. Carolyn has been a God-given gift to us. I know she was to you. We both were overwhelmed with how to approach your works but began plotting our strategy. Her years of teaching writing, her invaluable expertise, and her willingness to organize and word process your writings has been immeasurable. We have shared much laughter, as well as shared our grief together, on the loss of a profound young writer at a much too early age. I always love to hear her saying, "My, oh my, I wish I would have said that," when she read or found particular meaningful words of wisdom you wrote! Through our journey together and long days of sorting and laughing we celebrated your life. I would spend hours and days, and now years, trying to decipher and transcribe your handwriting. I knew in my heart and could hear you yell at me if I changed any form or words. I'm writing you, my son, to say we did eventually figure out every word. Carolyn formatted each piece in the form that you had hand-written your poetry or prose. The titles to each chapter are phrases we found as "one liners" throughout your writings. Your journals are printed in italics followed by other prose and poetry. Many of the writings in your book are untitled. Carolyn and I contemplated giving them titles! We didn't Spenser. Trust your mother!

When Carolyn brought over the first word-processed pieces, my heart, soul and mind reacted with joyous feelings for then I could truly see and read your works with a clearer understanding. That was the turning event of making your later life's work into a book.

The book will never replace you or the love and experiences our family and friends could have shared with you. But I thank you for leaving us the written work. We have your stories now that we cherish. It is a precious and priceless gift to us. I can now lay to rest some part of my grief that there will never be any more written Spenser stories. I hear your words to me during your last days of life as you wanted so much to be with Jesus, "Mother, don't cry,"as I wept at your bedside. Spens, I don't cry for you but I still cry for me, Dad, Sage and Sam because we miss you and the dynamics you played in our family.

Not too long after you left us, Dad and I found a turn-of-the-century, dark oak vestment chest at an estate sale. Hand-carved on the outside front is
"GRACE ME AND GUIDE
LOVE YE ONE ANOTHER."
Some of your favorite earthly belongings are in the vestment chest — your baseball cards, baseball bat,

books, sweaters, leather jacket, pictures of friends, etc. Now, your handwritten writings will be put to rest there also.

For the first six years of your life at Lake Quivira, Kansas, you and I had our favorite story spot on the bottom stoop of the stairs leading to our upstairs. Your make-believe companion was Johnny. We shared and made up stories about dunnies (fish), gummies (horses), M & Ms and your favorite things. Oftentimes we anchored ourselves on the point along the grassy slope of the lakeshore by our home and as we fished, we told stories. Sometimes when I went to bed at night you and Dad stayed up late and I overheard the stories you two shared.

You were in first grade when we moved to the country near Ottawa, Kansas. Sage was two years old and Sam was nine years old. Our lives and stories expanded to your love of the creatures found in the creek along our property, trapping skunks in the woods, raising your dogs, chickens, rabbits, homing pigeons, horses, sheep, and orphaned creatures. You ran like a deer exploring our woods and we played catch in the front yard many days. Always, at bedtime, Dad or I said your prayers with you, and we told stories about the day's events.

Years have passed in our lives since you were here with us. A day never passes that I don't think of you. We're really doing fine, though. We still laugh, love, and get mad at each other! Through Sage's "growing up" years you marveled at her and admired her. Now she is an admirable college woman attending the University of Vermont. Sam is a fourth year medical student at Harvard and married to Diane

Hotten, a graduate student at Boston College. We open our hearts to her in our circle of love. Dad is with Dorsey & Whitney and works as diligently as ever. I'm the one who now has a marvelous job as an Assurance of Mastery Teacher for grades 3-5 at Highlands in Edina. You know what I love the very best about my work besides the children? Telling them stories . . .

Spenser, I thank you for giving us your words of wisdom and the legacy you have left us of your words and stories. You know I love you and miss you. But I know too you must know in your heavenly home all these things that I've now written to you. I found the Bible passage 1 John 4:12 underlined in your Bible: "No one has ever seen God, but if we love each other God lives in us and His love is made complete in us."

I love you,
Mom

Mom

Acknowledgments

My greatest thank you is to Spenser for his legacy of written thoughts and words. To my dear husband, John, who understood the commitment in getting Spenser's writings organized, and for the grief and joy he shared with me in doing so. To my dear children, Sam and Sage, I hope that the time and solitude I needed while organizing Spens' writing did not take time away from you and your companionship. I thank you for your love.

Kathy Buller Kirchhoff, a long-time friend, said, "Karen, you *do have* time to work on Spens' writings, at least one hour at a time." Her prompting helped me to reach my goals. Lisa Yates said, "Read to me, whenever and whatever you have of Spenser's." I will always cherish her time and caring spirit given to Spenser's book, as well as, her encouragement and friendship to me. Carolyn Rebholz's dedication, commitment, and writing expertise immensely helped in making this book a reality. Connie Anderson made certain all the "t's" were crossed and the "i's" dotted. Thank you friends.

John and I are also thankful to Spenser's friends who come by and share their lives and "Spenser stories and experiences" with us: Chris Davis, Neil Johnson, Kurt Vickman, Ryan Lund, Danny Arom, Clark Schumacher, Eugene Munster, Joe Cavanaugh, and Lesley McBurney who also shared Spenser's letters for this book. Jeff Northrup wrote and recorded on his album, *North of Sixty,* a song "To a King" in honor of Spenser. We also thank all Spenser's 1990 Edina High School classmates for their memorial contributions.

Thanks also to Spenser's teachers at Valley View Junior High and Edina High School, Edina, Minnesota, who always understood that his health and recovery time were more important than his presence in the classroom. We especially thank Joan Schulz, Spenser's creative writing teacher, who organizes the Spenser Somers Memorial Guest Author Series each year at Edina High School.

Thanks too to the many doctors, nurses, and health care providers who cared for and about Spenser. Especially, I thank Drs. Bruce Bostrom, Stacy Robeck, Kenneth Heithoff, and the late Dr. Larry Singher, Spens' trusted oncologist and friend who together shared the joys of living, as well as, fears of cancer.

Last but not least, we send our prayers of thanks to Spenser's spiritual friends: Pam Loffhagen, Spens' spiritual director; Pastor Dean Nadasdy, for his creative gifts of writing which influenced Spenser as he listened and learned from him from confirmation to death; and Barbara Davis, for her gift of song and humor.

– Karen Somers

Prologue

I want the words
>to be snow.

I want the snow
>to be sculpted
>into something
>tangible,
>real, beautiful.
>A snowman
>formed in the
>endless tundra
>of the mind.

I want the words
>the snow,
>to be scooped up and
>sculpted into something real,
>tangible,
>beautiful.

A snowman
>formed inside
>the tundra of the mind.

I want my words to be snow.

Snow, to be sculpted into something
>real,
>tangible
>something beautiful.

• • •

A snowman formed by mittens
        inside the tundra
        of the mind.
I will no longer write in words.
        Instead
Snowflakes will emerge from the
        end of my pen.
Tiny snowflakes.
They will fall effortlessly onto
        the paper.
They won't discriminate anywhere
        in the script.

Destinations can be reached regardless of the pace

his journal is sacred for many reasons. Most of all it shows how I am and who I was. All the poems, stories are old adolescent thoughts immortalized on paper that shall forever live even when I'm cold beneath the ground with my soul soaring where the mortals can only dream of. Hopefully! It scares me to think that time, the thing taken most for granted in the world, can have its limitations. But we shall all die. But this book, along with other miscellaneous words, shall long walk on this earth when I'm soaring above. Pressure and frightening thoughts bring me to say all of this, but we can always read my thoughts of old and with the press of the button we can recall the thoughts of Elton John, Cat Stevens, Billy Joel, and even the Beastie Boys, for the thoughts of humans are only important for a few moments. And we must hold sacred those times cherishing the ones we love while there is still time for our arms to wrap around the ones we love. So hold precious the times to love and to hate for time can be *raped from us with the blink of an eye.*

Discover early what is important to you. Smiles, laughter, tears are gifts of God to be enjoyed while there is still time to hold them close to your heart. So never cry without laughing, for time can be lost as easily as your keys to your car.

I love you. Everyone, Smile. Laugh. Cry. Enjoy your life for life is definitely too short. But God still smiles. And so do I.

Sure I wish I could write down everything I'm feeling toward everyone. But I can't. And the emotions you receive from a kiss, a sunrise, an "A," or "Good-bye Yellow Brick Road," can only become words with meaning. And please accept my words, not as wisdom, but as meaningful. As meaningful as a kiss, a sunrise, an "A," or even "Good-bye Yellow Brick Road."

And always smile! God's eyes shall forever watch over you and his hand will guide you. Keep your head viewing the heavens and your hand open. For soon you shall dance eternally with him.

Dedication continued . . .

A wise man out east set his
       book of philosophy aside and
       set off to find true answers.
A well-dressed angel who never
       wore a halo because it messed
       up her hair dropped her shopping
       bags and fluttered out of a shopping
       mall. She'd go somewhere where the
       gift of love was being shared.
A shepherd awoke from one of his many
       naps and walked with his hands in his
       pockets to where he heard soft thoughts.
A king left his courtroom, grabbed a
       sack full of gold, hopped onto his red
       horse and rode looking for a place
       to give his gifts.
They had no star to guide them. They
       followed the lights inside their hearts.
Somehow their internal compass led them
       to the frigid cold of Minnesota. They gathered
       outside a hotel upon a dew-filled hill.
       They were hesitant whether to go in
       and just as the wise man was about
       to convince them how irrational this
       whole ordeal was and that they should all
       return to from where they had come,

           . . .

a jolly innkeeper opened the door.
"Come in from the cold. My inn has
many vacancies."
When they entered, they all realized they'd found
what they were searching for, inside that house
on that cold winter night. The wise man
found his answers,
and his mind was content. The angel found
the free gift of love
being shared. The shepherd received new
energy, and the
king gave his gold.
Everything that they had come for
was realized the moment they felt
the great love of the house, which
was kept warm by the innkeeper's love.
They set gifts upon a fir tree
that stood tall clothed with its ornaments.
Beneath the tree was a creche
with the baby Jesus.
The jolly innkeeper smiled saying, "It takes
a lotta' love to make Christmas, Christmas."
Their hearts brimmed with joy as they
felt the incredible love.

When the walk of life gets tiresome, that's when you should stop walking and simply dance.

Words weave unintelligible
       through mazes of the mind.
Some escape, yet they
       love to wander aimlessly.
Playing games. They refuse
       to be trapped,
       imprisoned in the bare white paper.
So this mischievous laughter
       rings through your head.
Pencils snap.
Cigarettes ignite.
They have won.
For now.

So much to write about:
       Gentle eyes.
       Quivering tresses.
Soon, soon images shall find
       their home upon paper.
Let that time not be taken from
       me.
Please.

The fruits of life are eaten with joy

The songs of the soul are all performed
      in harmony. Hymns to soothe. Rock 'n
      Roll to celebrate. Poetry with rhythm.
God touches those who reach for
      him. He must hold your heart
      before grasping your hand.
Digest the fruits and join the
      choir praising the Lord.

The winter's cold is
      a lonely cold.
The midnight sky is barren for the
      cold seems to disperse the
      clouds leaving the rich blue naked.
The road narrowed to one lane. The
      snow drifts trying to engulf
The mud and gravel and spread
      the white in its greedy ways.
The cows huddle together in an asymmetrical
      design. Each cow selfishly finding
      heat from the others, not camaraderie
      just instinctive survival tactics for
      personal gain.
But the farmhouse with its warm breath
      becomes a haven.

Endless roads, new horizons

I want to play the guitar
    and sing to dancing people
    on a street corner.
My hair will keep my shoulders
    happy with its company.
I'll have comfortable jeans that won't leave my legs.
I'll buy a motorcycle that
    will carry my solitary
    soul to happy places, piercing
    the air and humming a melody
    that will keep me and the
    endless road company.

The highways stretched and rolled, sloped and
changed names, but kept going on and on.
    It's bringing me home
    Away from the hugeness
    to the simplicity of a windmill pumping
    water and roosters waking the sun.
    The red barn where the chickens
    resided lost color. And the pictures
    of home where the memories were
    leaving and losing color
    So slowly it seemed illegal.

Shadows of the night

Walking the streets alone,
It's dark, but fear has long since
      passed.
Shadows of the night prey on lesser
      beings, when shadows combine. It
      only strengthens the darkness.
No, tonight I shan't be harmed.
So I walk on, thinking only of what
      must be done.
The dark streets are brightly lighted, now.
I see young girls with torn down
      sanctuaries.
No love in their eyes, only hate in
      their hearts,
But they survive, struggling to keep
      their minds free from the nightmare of
      reality that surrounds them.
I walk on.
A man stands before me who specializes in
      keeping the reality as far from the mind
      as possible.
He is only doing a service, much like a bartender.
His customers think his products help them survive,
      but in the end, he is the only one surviving
      off their ignorance.
I am almost there.
I turn into an alley.   ...

It reeks of trash; filth is everywhere.

A man sits in a corner, sucking a bottle long since
        dry.

He does not survive; he himself has become trash,
        only waiting to be carried away and burned.

I pass the alley.
        Now I have reached destination.

I step inside
        Reach into my pocket and I find my survival
        weapon.

The clerk senses danger, but remains calm.
        He, like all the others, becomes a slave to
        my power.

Fast money from an unwilling source.
        It's easy, and I survive.

The law does not always help the real people.
        So sometimes you must help yourself.

Some may call me a shadow of the night, but I, like so
        many others, am a survivor.

Helping myself to the gluttony of others.

My jeans keep fading

My jeans keep fading
As the world goes on hating
It's time to walk on water
It's time to walk on water
Dance upon the sky
The only blues I want are
        the ones in your eyes.
Walking alone down the road
I'm tired of the tears
the somer-salting years
the screaming, the pain, the cries
All those that despise
and cling to their fears
My jeans keepa' fading
My jeans keepa' fading
Becoming a softer blue
Tell ya' where I'm going
        It's time to
Walk on the water
Walk on the water
        It's time to

• • •

Dance upon the sky
Tell all the sadness good-bye.
The birds keep singing
The church bells ringing
The wind tells its tales
As we follow our trails
I wish we could listen
        and hear what we're missing
By screaming at each other
Instead of calling 'em brother
Walkin' barefoot through the meadow
        of my mind
I leave the sickness of darkness
        behind.

Destination somewhere
traveling nowhere

The steel snake slithered on
Cutting through mountains and
under bustling crowded streets.
Never seeing the majestic
rocky cliffs, antelope gnawing
lush green grass of the smiling
children playing marbles in a
grade school playground.
The steel beast surrounded by
cold concrete and traveling
on a predetermined path that
is guided by a man that
has nothing but a schedule
that must be kept and a
destination that must
be reached so that the
nothingness can be replaced
by the land above.
Sleep brings another day.
Another day of responsibility
And obstacles that must
be overcome. So why sleep?

A woman driving, smiled
as she contently waited
for a family of ducks
to change lanes and then
cross to the lake.
She came to the stop sign.
He came and stopped
after her.
He drove away
Before she did.
She laid on the horn.
Honking like a goose
at the Red Chevy which
took her place and
made her late.

Freshly showered
Tension, but still manageable
Happy faces met with happier faces.
Slow ride, but happy ride.
Destination.
Stay in tension-filled car
with a tension-filled person.
Greetings, welcomes follow
Fun and games followed by
more fun and games.
Games which I'm a
spectator.
"Let's cruise."
They follow.
Silence and rage multiplying
more silence and rage.

*ife seems to be rushing by lately. I've felt like I've been standing in line at the bus stop for the wrong bus. Even when the right bus finally comes along, I all too often let it pass simply because I know another MTC will be coming soon enough today, though I didn't wait for a ride, instead, started walking to where I wanted to go.*

I'm tired.

Today I really began to realize how important every day is and there's no sense in procrastinating. There are no limits to how many smiles you can share in a single day. Love knows no boundaries, a heart can never be too full. Dreams are as realistic and obtainable as you yourself, make them. That's what it all boils down to I guess, is that a person has to truly work for what he/she wants.

If you want cash, you gotta get a good job — even if you want to be happy, you must concentrate upon the good instead of the bad. Where did all this come from??? My God! I'm talking in cliches! Like I said — it's late.

Maybe I'm becoming responsible, wah, never!!

June 9, 1990

Graduation address

Well, in the words of Martin Luther King, Jr., "We are free at last, oh free at last." We've finally made it. I joked with my mother earlier that the only graduation and commencement ceremony I might ever attend could be my funeral, but I made it. Just as one leg cannot walk by itself, a single wing cannot fly and one hand cannot clap by itself, I did not get here alone. I finally get to thank some of those people who were my extra legs when I needed to walk, the extra wings when I needed to fly, and the hands that were constantly applauding and cheering me to get here.

First and foremost, I want to thank my heavenly Father, the giver of all life, creator of all, with whom all things are possible. Since it is graduation, I guess He could be likened to the superintendent of the highest school and who has let me stay enrolled in my, or rather His, earthly classroom for longer than most of the doctors thought possible.

I'd also like to thank publicly my great family, Mom, Dad, Sam, Sage. I love you guys, and all my friends outside of school for all their support and prayers.

That brings me to you all, the incredible class of 1990. There is little doubt in my mind that without your loving, kind, generous and rowdy spirit that I would not be here today. And I thank you.

That spirit could be seen at all the sporting events both competing and cheering in the stands.

The spirit that brought in 1,000's of can goods for the needy.

The same spirit that every time they would see Troy, a mentally retarded boy at school, they would give him a high five and tell him what they were going to do that night.

That same spirit that in this very arena hopped over the hockey boards and onto the ice and hoagied on the hockey team for the first time in Edina's history.

That same spirit that would grab their lawn chairs, radios, hot dogs, and potato chips and have barbecues upon the hill during varsity baseball games.

That same spirit that named a skinny, bald guy with jokes almost as bad as his haircut as their Homecoming King.

That spirit has given me so many smiles, so many hugs, so much to laugh about. High fives, not to mention prayer—oops—not to mention well, prayer too, not to mention pencils and lunch money. And just as during the Homecoming Coronation you gave me a standing ovation, I can finally give you one. So class of 1990 you have my deepest thanks and in a true Somers' fashion and to lighten the mood, I give you my standing O—Thanks a lot. I wasn't going to do that but there was somebody reading a book over there before.

Well, as my new brown curls attest to, it has been a hair raising experience. Seriously though, we learned a lot, as school is truly intended. Besides facts and figures and numbers and other stuff, we learned other things besides those. Here are a few things good ol' EHS has taught, at least tried to teach, me and the Class of '90. I mean the Class of '90 and I!:

We learned the difference between getting things done and truly accomplishing something.

Mr. Lynch with his unique perspective on all

things taught us that janitors weren't janitors at all but engineers.

We learned that the bond of friendship is stronger than any ionized bond or hydrogen bond could ever be.

We learned the value of sadness and tears and the pricelessness of happiness and laughter.

You all taught me that a smile on the face is a lot more important than hair upon the head.

We learned that most teachers were not only human, but some of the most sincere, caring people around, genuine priests without the collar.

We learned that our rivals, the Minnesota Skippers, may have the lake, but we have the boats. Which reminds me, I don't think we ever did find out what a skipper was.

We learned that before you write a paper or give a speech you had better have something to say.

And Officer Friendly of the Edina Police Department taught us homecoming court members that the little green light means you pass, the little yellow is a warning, and the red light means you are in big trouble. I knew we'd all laugh about that some day.

And through it all, you guys have taught me the greatest lesson of all that love not only touches people's lives, but can pick them up and carry them to places thought unattainable, like behind a podium at a high school graduation.

And through it all, I hope I've taught you guys a thing or two, like how precious each day is. I guess I used to think that life was like a long highway. I pictured myself in an old Mustang convertible with the top down, the wind blowing through my hair; a pair of black Ray Bans on and listening to classic rock and roll. I was just cruising along on what I thought at the time to be an endless road. I, however, got stuck with a faulty engine. It forced me to stop cruising, and to pull over onto the shoulder and start walking. And it was once I started walking that I began to see all the beauty that was only a colorful blur before. Once I began to walk, the wind didn't blow through my hair, 'cause I didn't have any, and instead of the music of the Beatles, it was the songs of the birds and the crickets to be heard. But once I started to walk and once I took off my shades I began to see things clearly for the first time. I began to see that success should not be measured by grades or dollar signs, but by how often you laugh or by how many people you can make smile in a day. I began to see that once you are at peace with God, peace with your fellow man comes, as well as peace with yourself. And I began to see that our earthly highway not only has plenty of detours and pot holes, but it isn't nearly as long as I once thought.

Now at graduation, when our futures are burning so brightly we hear phrases like "You have your whole life ahead of you." To those I argue that you've had your whole life, and all that you have is today. So when you feel your life is going too fast, or you are just cruising along, pull over onto the shoulder or exit on the nearest ramp and start walking. Start seeing what you're missing and better yet, start laughing at all those stressful sports cars zipping by. Because in a marginal pun, if you're in the fast lane, the passing lane, you are not in the right lane. Once we stop looking up the road for peace and satisfaction and start looking around for it, that's when it will come.

Class of 1990, thank you and good luck on whatever path your feet walk upon.

Today soon to be tomorrow

*D*ear Journal, when I embarked on a
journey of words back in October, I had
no idea where it would take me, but as
always, journeys must end. And on this
April evening, Today Soon to Be Tomorrow shall be written
into for the final time.

*The book, as my life, has come a long way. Love was
found only to be lost. Basketball season as did Christmas,
came and went. Stories were told, poems recited, but just as
the present soon becomes the past, the words shall forever live
their lives in this book. I'm sure they will like their residency,
for I'm the one who gave them their home. There will be, with
God's help, more books written into, but this one will always
have its unique character, for it is who I am, and who I was,
and just as there will be changes in my outlook on life, this
book will always be a foundation to look back on, reminding
what I am, or was.*

*All the words written in here are first drafts, straight
from my mind to the paper. So just remember that minds are
never "fully perfect." I wanted to have a "grand finale" poem
or story that would completely awe the reader, but the words,
as so often happens, did not come to me tonight. So I keep
searching, hoping that one day that story, novel, or poem will
be birthed. I don't think anyone likes to say good-bye, but
everything comes to a close. Humans are very greedy and try
to refuse that fact, but nevertheless logic can't be argued with.
The few pages I leave blank, naked, symbolize that nothing
can ever be truly finished, and that my literary battles have
just begun and will never end, but they walk.*

Goodbye . . .

A smile with a giggle, that's what life should be

Ahh, the sound of laughter, it is definitely a purifying experience. It brings a sense of euphoria that can be likened to active meditation. *I believe it is a form of prayer, and what is better for our unclean spirits than a prayer filled with a couple of good giggles. Laughter's over-whelming feeling of giddiness clears the mind of evil thoughts, and the person is left smiling and temporarily enlightened. Laughter not only brings us closer to God and others, but I have a hunch that the flowers' buds open simply because they want to absorb the wonderful sound.*

Smile, for tomorrow's light comes quickly.

Eating LIFE® cereal with a bigger spoon than most

Bright light, combining with the chilling sound of my mother's voice, brought my dreaming subconscious to reality. The reality of morning. "Phillip, it's 7:35! Get up!" she screamed. I didn't need to open my eyes to see what I'd seen so many times before — her standing in the door, hands on hips, fire in her eyes, wanting in her heart for her irresponsible child to wake from the dead and rise in time to make it before the first tardy bell.

I remained silent, clutching the sheets, seeking their warmth and refusing to relinquish the pleasure of sleep. Mother hated it when I didn't acknowledge her screams or the fact that I would be late to school for the third time this week. Maybe my silence was a whacked-out sort of revenge for my rude awakening. "7:36!! Get up. NOW!!" The angered, frustrated voice now traveling from down the hall.

I glanced at my clock. It was a trick she sometimes used — to lie about the time. She had tried every trick in the book to abort me from the warm womb of my bed. Few worked. My clock was blank. I had unplugged it late last night. I didn't need the evil digital numbers glowing in the dark to know that tomorrow would come. The morning sun coming, as always, too quickly. My philosophy was: sleep brings another day, another day of responsibility and obstacles to overcome, so why sleep? Instead make the day as long as possible. Indeed, that's what I'd done last night. I stayed up extremely late, thinking and writing mostly. I seemed to receive my creative genius from the content stillness of the midnight sky and the moon's mellow light.

I pursed my lips in a lackadaisical smile. (I always tried to start the day and end the day with a smile.) And slowly let my mind adjust to the new day. I didn't let myself succumb to the sweet, enticing whisperings that would draw me back to the wistful waters of sleep. Not today, I was late enough as it was. I peeled the sheets from my tired body and decided to venture into the waters of a shower instead.

Picking my path carefully through the random articles of clothes and trash in my room, I entered into the hall. Walking with my eyes open as little as possible so as not to let too much light enter them, I passed my younger sister in the hall. "Good morning," she said. I didn't look up, but she was probably smiling. Her elementary school didn't even start for another hour. Definitely a morning person. A terrible thing to be. Someday all the night owls of the world will unite and attack. Swooping down they will maim all morning people, or at least gouge out their eyes to make their victims live in eternal darkness. I raised a benevolent, limp hand to acknowledge her existence, saving vengeance for the birds, and proceeded to the bathroom for my daily cleansing.

I opened the shower door, turned the knob and tested the water. Cold, extremely cold. That's one of the hassles when living with morning people. The last one up received no hot water; they refer to it as an incentive deal. I call it another one of their tricks to get me to school on time.

Lenard, my older, concrete sequential brother (I was the middle child, of course), got the first shower every day. Every day since puberty brought its greasy hair; he was the first one in the shower. He probably sang in the shower, or in his case, hummed a symphony. Sinful, absolutely sinful. My father usually took the second shower, stealing the last precious drops of hot liquid as well. He wasn't exactly a morning person or a night owl. Many a night he burned the midnight oil, not because he was a night owl, but because of his work. He was a corporate attorney. A lifetime of long nights, stress-filled days, lack of exercise, and Camel Lights had brought executive success, but I wondered how happy he was. A kind, generous man. All the work hadn't hardened his heart at all. A hot shower was the least I could sacrifice for him. I often wondered if that was all I gave him, especially since he had given me so much.

I jumped in the shower, eyes closed, jaw clenched, and washed my hair in under thirty seconds.

"7:43! Phillip, hurry!" Mom screamed from downstairs. First hour starts in 17 minutes. Looks like I'll be late again. Mr. Sandersen, my geometry teacher, won't be happy. Oh well, one more hour of detention didn't matter. Mr. Sandersen didn't care for my laid-back style too much. He referred to me as "Mr. Lazy." Geometry teachers lack creativity even in their put-downs. Once I had asked him if his parallel line had ever intersected his wife. No laughter, just another hour of detention. Geometry teachers lacked humor as well.

I searched my chest of drawers for some fashion treasures, finding none, I grabbed a white t-shirt. I slipped on a pair of faded jeans from off the floor and headed for breakfast.

I sauntered into the dining room. My sister, Jenny spoke, "About time. You're going to be late. Again!" She laughed, obviously amused with her great knowledge. That's one thing about little sisters, not only are they masters of the obvious, but they think they know it all too. I paid no attention to her being and sat next to Lenard who had eaten his breakfast and was reading the paper.

Mom, donning her worn bathrobe and tired slippers, pointed a finger filled with disappointment towards the table and said, "Eat."

Directly ahead of me sprawled not only my cereal but the rest of the kin's as well. Jenny had her Cap'n Crunch. I remember my Cap'n Crunch stage. Elementary school days always began with good 'ol Cap'n Crunch. I switched to Life during junior high. I've never been too crazy for the taste, but the humor in the idea of controlling Life with a spoon, and the thought of "eating Life" struck me funny. Len's bowl had only a few Grape Nuts left, looking more like pebbles in a white lake than something edible. I don't' think he ever had a Cap'n Crunch stage, or Life for that matter. I sure hope I never get caught in a Grape Nuts rut.

Drink from a full cup

Dance to the bird's song.
Touch the wind.
Keep your feet on the ground.
Your hands searching for the sky.
Leave your eyes open to feel
       the earth's breath.
Sing your own song.
Laugh until you cry.
Let the river of tears flow
       over your smile.
Find love in each day.
Dreams should be contained inside
       closed eyes, never sleeping minds.
Dream with your eyes open. The
       sun's light and watery tears
       nourish inner growth.
Dream with your whole soul. Making
       your being a pleasant forecast.
Climb mountains driving your car.
Find fair maidens with white veils
       and red rubies for eyes while
       sitting in your room.
Dream. Every day.
Dream 'til you've laughed with the wind
       and have smiled with the sun.

Bugs — they make up such a big part of the eco-system. Nothing a little Raid Yard Guard couldn't fix. They say cockroaches will survive a nuclear explosion. Think of that as a new race in conversion of the world. Night time would be their active time. They are going to work riding on the backs of VW Beetles and Bugs. Then when the sun rises, they scamper off to live in houses. They would sculpt the rocks into condos. But for the very rich cockroaches, they'd live inside humans' houses. Inside cabinets. But the humans, the remaining ones would be caught and killed with yep, you guessed it, Human Heels.

I just read what I wrote last night . . . I was pretty tired and even though I tried to say some cool stuff, I don't think it turned out very well. Like I said I was pretty tired . . .

SAM got into DARTMOUTH!! I found out today in the hall. I was sooo happy for him. He is so excited! His life is set. I hope the best for him — he'll go far.

Got a math test tomorrow and biology — shitty.

Yellow eye

My mom made eggs for breakfast, cyclops'
        yellow eye in a white feathered face stared
        at me. I had to look away. Now
        the huge yellow eye peered at me from the
        trash can. Parts of its face pasted
        against yesterday's newspaper. It looked
        like an anatomy experiment
        gone bad. The nose, protruded
        from the want ads. The trash man
        took the eye and face away. I could
        picture the yellow tears staining the
        feathery white.
A boy looked too long at his eggs today. Instead
        of throwing them to the trash, he hopped
        in and waited for the trash man. His face
        decorated with tiny metal balls. His
        nose nowhere to be seen. The trash man
        took him away. I saw the red tears, not from
        his eyes, staining his body.

A little boy broke from
　　　　his protective mother's side
　　　　as they were rushing across
　　　　a soaked grocery parking lot.
　　　　He had spotted a puddle that seemed
　　　　to be calling his name and wanted
　　　　to have the juvenile's feet placed
　　　　into it.
　　　　"Joey, come back!"
He stared, eyes still focused upon
　　　　the social gathering of
　　　　rain that was so tempting.
　　　　He returned to his mother's
　　　　side only to have his
　　　　back side swatted.
　　　　"Puddles of rain will get you wet,"
　　　　she muttered.
The sky released a clap of
　　　　thunder that sounded more like
　　　　an old man giggling than anything
　　　　frightening.

Happy 20th birthday
(you know the date)

Sam—

I'm sorry I've invaded your thoughts/personal soul.

Again, I'm sorry. You must realize, however, I love your thoughts as well as your personal soul.

Thoughts are fun to play with. Enjoyment in the mind.

In the mind; or is it the soul? Of course, I want to bring you warm thoughts to set an inferno to your mind, but your mind is already aflame.

So I just want to bring you a . . . smile.

So please smile.

Realize, of course, the happiness in being Sam Somers.

For Sam is wonderful. (I hope you're smiling and not correcting my lack of grammar skills.)

I hope Taiwan brings no thoughts of loneliness, because loneliness is only the emotion of not being satisfied.

And satisfaction is rare. The only thing that brings satisfaction is contentedness. Truer peace.

Sam Somers, I hope you find the elusive smile of contentment. Of course, it is so rare; that elusive smile that lingers inside a searching mind.

Believe it when I say I'm not yet fully content. Full of a couple of beers, yes, content, however, no.

Sam, of course, you are realizing the potential inside of yourself. A potential that you'd never fully realize. But what the hell, we might as well try, eh?

I've stopped writing poetically to you and now saying what I mean.

It makes a lot more sense that way — no?

I see both of us following a path of frustration.

What can make us the most happy?

Ourselves.

Be happy Sam Somers.

And always smile.

Life, of course, is too short . . . smiles, however, never last long enough.

Maybe I shouldn't have said, however, but hell, squares and cubes can be as large or as small as the brain, or mind. Let them be.

As many thoughts can be crowded into squares, there are ideas dancing just a little bit beyond the perimeter of that square and to make a complete square world/thought you must expand the square to encompass that idea.

Pretty soon you have to expand the square, but there is always that idea hanging. So soon that square transforms to a circle.

But have you ever met someone who could draw a perfect circle? Think about that.

So what does this all mean? No shit. What does it mean? Is logic the answer? Is God the answer? (well, yes, but . . .)

Is irresponsible, happiness the answer?

I guess the only answer is well, yep, there is no answer. And once you've found the answer obviously

you've stopped listening to the questions.
> I love you,
> Your little brother

Keep Searching
> For God
> For yourself
> For smiles
> Find love. Find the unexplainable simplicity
> of love.
> Oh yeah.
> I love you.

Timothy

Timothy holding
Timothy jerking
Timothy and his mother
      walking through
      the Ottawa IGA parking lot.
Timothy's four sisters holding
      on to mother,
      his thumb and remnants
      of a grape jelly sandwich
      giving the congealed reassurance
      Timothy needed.
      Timothy, his free hand
      and eyes pointing up at the sky,
      "It's not going to rain today. No sky
      kleenex up there."
      "Hurry up, Timmy."
Timothy watching the macaroni
      and cheese disappear into a brown bag.
      Hearing the lady in the corner saying
      how nice a day it was.
      "Not even one kleenex."
      "That will be $38.50, please."
Timothy lying in bed with his
      nite-light revealing that
      his door was not left open
      turned and confided in
      Sammy, the giraffe,

                        ...

who did not get out much.
"The sky was happy today."
Sammy's one eye
sparkled as he said,
"Good. Thanks for
telling me."
Even with the exit
sealed the monsters didn't
have too much reason
to bother smiling
because little boys' dimples
keep monsters away
more than sunshine.

My sister wants to be a football
             star.
My brother wants to change the
             world.
I just walk slowly, hands in my
             pockets, face to the clouds
             and smile.
The fierce, cold winds have tried
             stealing the warmth from
             me many times.
I wear a thicker jacket than
             most; it's lined with many smiles.
I never wear a watch. I don't
             need sands of time to tell me
             tomorrow will come.
I love to play in the warmth
             of the ocean of life. Some
             drown. I never get wet.
I just walk slowly, hands in
             my pockets, face to the
             clouds and smile.

Going fishing

Benjamin Sanderson set his green plastic tackle box on the kitchen counter and opened the refrigerator. He opened the drawer marked "meat," the left one, and grabbed a package of hot dogs. They were the last article he needed before his fishing trip could begin. He fished with the yellow jig that was connected to his Zebco pole. The hot dogs were for nourishment and means.

"Benjamin, what are you doing?" It was his mother's tired voice. She didn't mind him taking hot dogs. It was the fishing part she disapproved of.

"Going fishing." He slid the hot dogs into his tackle box.

"Ben, is Leonard going with you?" Leonard was Ben's older brother. Leonard preferred a good book to bright sunshine or green grass any day.

"No." Ben for the first time looked at his mother. Even though he was young he had discovered that looking into someone's eyes helped one's cause a lot more than staring at the ground. His mother's eyes, however, were the hardest to look at. They were always so tired or even worse, sometimes had tears in them. Today her eyes did look tired. Her clothes were dirty from cleaning the house. A bandanna was tied around her head to keep her dark hair from her eyes.

"Mom, I'll be careful."

"Ben, please."

"I'll stay on our land."

"Be careful."

"Thanks!" Ben grabbed his tackle box and hurried out of the kitchen. His mom was saying

something about eating raw hot dogs and gas pain,
when the screen door and the bright Kansas sunshine
welcomed him.

Their black lab mixture mutt and he raced to
the blue shed. Benjamin was first to arrive in the
coolness of the barn, because the dog dropped out of
the race halfway and gave chase to a squirrel.

The barn was an antique store, a hardware store
and tack barn wrapped into one. It had as many
mysteries as it had mice. His fishing pole, a Zebco 026,
was patiently leaning against the dog food bin.
Leonard always teased Benjamin that their parents
named him so because he was full of dog food. Ben's
mom laughed, but since then she always called the
Dog Food Bin, The Dog Food Container.

*If love is so great, why can't we buy it
at Dayton's?*

If only the heart could overcome
      the mind, we all would smile.
When your world has only
      pain, sorrow, and tears,
      look back and remember
      all of its good years.
Remember the smile you
      brought to so many
      faces.
Forget about all the bad,
      For up your sleeve there have
      to be some aces.
Remember Krisy, Kristine, Jenni, Tyra,
      Jessica, Liz and Kim
      and your true friends.
      Because above all, friendship
      never really ends.
Remember Spaghetti-O's and
      wine.
Think back when everything
      was just fine.
Remember sleep-overs at
      Kristine's house.
And how we all had to
      be quiet as a mouse.
Remember the locket and the rose,
      And of your cute little
      toes.
Remember New Year's Eve
      and of our "wait."

                                      ...

Think of TG's and our very
     first date.
Remember the Bill
     and the boy called D.I.
Remember how Jacqui
     could play and B.H.
Remember the weekend when
     I had "sinned."
Remember our "moods and
     all the cool silly dudes."
Like Nick and Merch
     and Dan and Rugs.
Remember my hair so
     long, and "Stand By Me,"
     they sang.
Remember the jacket and hat,
     and how Molly and Twil
     thought they were fat.
Through your hard time, I hope
     you'll see,
     and remember me.

ello from study hall. Write this date on the calendar, yes Tuesday, April 11, 1989 Spenser Somers went to study hall! I've forgotten how fun they are.

We just filled out some sheet, or should I say shit, about what the average high schooler (me) worries about. I could feel the tension in the air when the sophomores (and juniors) heard the word pregnancy or AIDS. But I had to laugh. Life seems simple right now and worries few. I think it's spring that is causing my carelessness. And yes, it's snowing as we speak/read. It's extremely chilly. I wish this place had windows. I forgot, or rather, I couldn't find, my backpack today. I think I left it in Chapman's van. Bummer. Needless to say, I don't think too much will get accomplished. Oh well.

The teachers' lounge

SETTING: A lavishly decorated room containing an assortment of strobe lights, loud music, and teachers drinking, smoking and dancing. A sign on the wall reads: "Teachers' Lounge." A wet bar is located in the rear, where the scene takes place. A teacher is sitting at the bar having a drink, next to him is a man with his head in his arms lying on the table, obviously passed out. A young, well-groomed substitute enters carrying a few books. Completely overwhelmed, his eyes and mouth wide open, he takes a seat at the bar.

Teacher Number 1 (drink in front of him): "Hey, How ya' doin' kiddo. (As a friendly gesture, Teacher Number 1 hits the sub in the arm. The blow nearly knocks the substitute off the stool.) You must be new here. Well, it's my pleasure to welcome you to the greatest teachers' lounge ever."

Substitute (overwhelmed and confused): "Well thanks. At least, I think I mean thanks, and yes, yes I am new. (A little more confidently.) I'm Timothy Beavers, substituting for Mr. Dee Sect's biology class."

Teacher Number 1: "Well, glad to meetcha', Timmy. (Teacher Number 1 offers his hand, the substitute instinctively responds. Teacher Number 1 squeezes hard. The substitute winces.) I'm Mack Daniels, the English teacher and this here (pats the man next to him who is passed out) is our dear, beloved principal, Mr. Bob Bunk. (whispers) His name's Bunk, but right now I think we could call him DRUNK! (He roars with laughter, delighted with himself. Realizing the substitute was not laughing, Teacher Number 1 composes himself.) Say, what's your pleasure?"

Substitute: "What?"

Teacher Number 1: "What shall I have the bartender getcha'?"

Substitute (shocked): "I don't drink, besides I have to teach a class in forty-five minutes. (Forceful, almost shouting, realizing the seriousness of the matter.) How can you call yourself a teacher? I mean, look at this place. Teachers dancing, smoking, playing quarters and look (points his finger towards the audience completely appalled), there are two people playing STRIP POKER!"

Teacher Number 1: "Oh don't worry about them none. It's just Mr. Sanchez the Spanish teacher and Mrs. Croissant the French teacher. Nothing wrong with them, just European is all."

Substitute (completely outraged, screaming): "I don't care who or what they are, this is an outrage!! This whole place is an outrage!! This is an embarrassment to the teaching profession! This is crazy! (He slams his books down and hysterically screams.) I Quit!!!!" (He stomps out.)

Teacher Number 1 (calmly addresses the audience, chuckles, shrugs his shoulders and says): "Boy, kids today sure are strange." (He then returns to his drink shaking his head.)

Spenser's homemade brew

Supplies bought

Total price $51.95

1st Batch

Mountmellick/Ireland

Export Ale

9:00 P.M. — recipe completed

Bottling date — Sept. 18

Drinking date (est.) — Nov. 5

Number of beers (est.) — 50 bottles

2 cases

I mixed everything right in the 5-gallon bucket, including 2 lbs of brewers sugar; could be a mistake.

(Still need bottles and to ask how much the Mountmellick cost.)

I shared with Sam some drunken
        wisdom tonight.
Cat Stevens still spreads
        his thoughts with the guitar.
The leather jacket still smelled
        the same.
Ryan still laughed.
Lesley's hair is still as
        red.
And God still smiles.
Time still passes in its
        casual manner.
My bed is still
        as soft.
Drunken wisdom becomes
        a headache the following
        day.
Cat Stevens' thoughts can
        be raped with a press
        of a button.
Ryan's laughter can be
        transformed into
        tears as easily as Lesley's hair
        can be changed.
But God still smiles.
Time changes with the
        coming of summer.
The cowhide can become
        as smelly as a stale
        spittoon. And a soft bed can be
        a strong river bed.
But God remains the same, a
        smile on the face.

So laugh, not only is it purifying, but you just might be opening a couple of flowers in the deal.

When I was child
Laughter always echoed in my ears.
I knew smiles and freedom.
The forest held so many mysteries.
      Secrets wanting to be known.
Hours consumed by solemn detective work.
Now the forest, a group of lonely trees,
      waits to hear the child's laughter which
      sits trapped inside of maturity!

Spenser (w/an s) that's me
Your name (w/a smile) that's you!
A smile (w/a giggle) that's what
      life should be.

Sit down, take a deep breath, and simply exist for a while

*H*ey Journal! Let's write! About what? I have no idea, but I'm writing whatever comes into mind. Ideas, thoughts, like my eyes, burn inside me. Waiting. Waiting to set an inferno that will light up the world, like a smile that spreads over a land, empty land bringing happiness and contentment.

Contentment.

White, the hare's tail
White, the doe's behind
White, the aspen tree
White, the gifts of God,
For all to see.

Red, clay to build
Red, sun to shine
Red, skin of Indians
Red, flood of liquid.

The great Spirit,
Make my skin the red tone
of earth, and the
light of the sun.

Peaceful drops of rain fell softly onto the
green grass, their oblong, thin tongues
stretching as far as
their roots would let them
to lap up the liquid that filled
them with such contentment.

ey journal!
HAPPY THANKSGIVING!
I'm not feeling too creative,
so I'm going to fill you in on what's
been happening in my life.
I made the basketball team. My life sure would have been
easier if I didn't. It's such a big commitment and I don't
know if my body is ready for it. I don't have the talent or the
same "killer instinct" I used to have. I don't have that drive
to excel athletically like I used to. It almost seems like I'm
wasting my time, especially when I could be going to ESSE,
or making some money. I also notice that I haven't written
much. Oh well, wish me luck.

On Tuesday of this week I had surgery. It wasn't
anything major, just to remove my portacath (a special "IV"
they implanted inside my chest so they wouldn't have to poke
me so much when I was going through chemo). Being "put
under" is a real experience. You hear this loud buzzing noise.
Then it feels like the base of your spine is staked down to the
table. It's funny because the process takes about two minutes
and I've been through it so many times (5 I think) that I
seemed to analyze the whole situation this time. Right before
I was unconscious, I wiggled my toes and then smiled.
I think I freaked them out a little. My arm still hurts a little,
but should be good as new in a few days.

Mom and Dad are still here too.

We yell a lot, but I'm mostly at fault. I love them a lot,
but sure do show it in a weird way.

My friend-situation is really weird right now. I seem
to go my separate way and they theirs; it doesn't really bother
me. Ryan probably my best friend right now, and he is
probably the best friend anyone could have.

Well, it was nice rappin with ya'. Thanks, and I'll
keep you posted. Wish me luck and help the rest of this book
to turn out some hot poetry!

Thoughts and images of you
        dance upon the setting
        sun and walk atop
        the glistening waters inside
        my mind.
But I await your return
        seated on the shoreline
        my toes receiving warm licks
        from the sea's puppy-like
        tongues. My heart so endeared to you,
        relying on my eyes, the images of you,
        to find the eternal fire.
If you, my love, dance upon the
        waters whose shape is being
        sliced by the land and melted by the sea
        with each blink of the eye, you must always
        flee before the darkness.
        Before the water has cooled
        the immense heat for a day.
Dancing in the dark I could
        never see you from
        my spectatorship. A title I earned;
        we earned together.
        Dancing in the dark. No.

                                     ...

You may find another blind, lonely soul
       to accompany your heart,
       traveling to someone else's
       ocean to perform upon their
       star of life.
I would sit, desperate, eyes searching
       the heart. The sea,
       now a grown, snarly beast, foaming
       striking again and again, never to mention
       me, not only toes, but my soul and
       only spirit as well.
See, honey lips, when the sun
       rises and when the moon's light
       and the star's guide walk
       atop the sea, join me seated
       on the shoreline. Please, after all,
       there's a volleyball net.

My bed, I forget how soft it
is. My stationary cotton
ball.
My window, shades open as
always. The city's lights
freckled upon a sleeping
black face.
Yes, I'm home. Home. How
wonderful it feels. Elton John
performs for me. My
tattered body securely placed
upon my bed. My eyes search
the sky for dancing thoughts.
A waltz, with the moon being the
band. The stars all dancing
slowly varying in intensity, yet
all swaying. They smile.
I'm home. Where else would I
rather be? Nowhere.
I'm home. My mind cluttered
and not thinking clearly.
Yet, I'm just getting warmed up.

Answers across the street

I t was in my first year (my first semester in fact) of studying Art Appreciation at the local university when I discovered the meaning of art. If I told you what it was at this moment, it would subtract from my story, so let's start from the beginning. It was one day after one of Professor Benson's more interesting sermons concerning art, the European classics centering around Michelangelo, when I confronted him with a heavy heart. It was not the presentation I was to inquire about, rather the assignment for the final he had bestowed upon our class two weeks earlier. The final was to represent in any way — literature, painting, song, photography, sculpture — what art means to you. This troubled me severely. I had no idea what to do. I was a business major and had taken the course upon a whim rather than out of necessity, but I had taken a liking to the class and did not want to do poorly on the final. I even looked forward to it every Wednesday and Friday at 9:00 in the morning.

As I said, however, I had no ideas for the final. I had spent many hours lying on my bed in my small dormitory, searching for an answer from the ceiling above. The answer refused to fall within my grasping mind and become my prisoner. The end of the grading period was a little more than a week away when I decided to see if I could possibly tap a few drops of knowledge concerning the final from Professor Benson's endless intellectual fountain.

So I wandered up to his immense old, oak desk for the confrontation. I was ill-prepared for the events to follow and was quite overwhelmed by his presence. The ancient desk and his ivory-tipped pipe, which filled the air with its unique fragrance, and had left its mark upon the Professor's teeth, seemed as much a part of him as the book his brown eyes were deeply focused upon. I waited until his eyes had acknowledged me and then spoke. "Excuse me sir, I have a question concerning the final."

He slowly laid his book aside, removed the pipe from his mouth, and a small smile rippled through his wrinkled face and softened his eyes as he said, "Yes. Paul, isn't it?"

"Yes."

"Very well, what is your question?"

As I stated earlier, I was quite ill-prepared and really didn't have a question but I did need an answer. I was nervous and completely at his mercy. I struggled to express my confused thoughts, but the words I mouthed were, "Well, ah, what do you mean?"

A chuckle, accompanying a sly, almost villainous smile, which did nothing for my state of mind, followed the question.

"Well Paul, what does art mean to you?"

Once more the blood refused to bring answers to my brain and the words evaded me. His brown eyes and brooding smile seemed to erase all rationality from my mind. He seemed to be toying with me, a game of cat and mouse where I was the mouse trapped in a corner waiting for the fatal blow to end it all. My cheeks burned with embarrassment as I shrugged my shoulders trying to escape his smiling face.

"Paul," he paused,"Where do you find great art?"

I was saved. He had given me safe exit and I could escape with at least some of my pride. "Well, a museum or art gallery, of course," I said.

"Well then, go there and find your answer," he said. He then gave me a smile and shooed me away with his hand, put his pipe once more in place, and gathered up his book.

I walked out feeling like a child, but nevertheless, he had given me a destination. I had tried to take the easy way out by going to him. It was like I had gone to the library looking for a book they didn't have and realizing I myself would have to write it, and so I headed off to the small art gallery that was located on campus to fulfill my quest.

I toured the small gallery for nearly two hours. It had a surprisingly good collection of art, some by artists on campus, but mostly by well-known American artists, both traditional and abstract. The place transmitted a weird sense of security and tranquility, but the question still echoed through my brain, "What does art mean to me?"

I was sitting on a wooden bench which they had supplied for the convenience of tired culture seekers, looking through a huge picture window at the park across the street when the answer hit me. Across the street, next to a huge willow tree was a solemn park bench. That one solitary bench gave me the answer my mind had been groping for. Aristotle once wrote that art is a moment forever frozen in time. At that moment, however, I came to know what art was to me. Art is an emotion transmitted by a single subject. Art can be found in everything and everything can be found in art. Art is not just a moment in time, but an emotion frozen in time. Everything seemed to come into focus. True love can be found in a picture, but the artist would have had to have known love in order to be inspired enough to relate the feeling to the viewer. Without emotion there would be no art, and without emotion the world would be boring, dismal, and lifeless, like walking in a circle with complete darkness. You would know what a circle was by walking it, but never know that a circle around a finger could signify love.

I still recall that day of new discovery and the "A" I received for my creative genius with great pleasure. And so I urge you, next time you're sitting in your room, in the shopping mall, kissing the one you love, or looking through a huge picture window, soak up all there is to see and let all the emotions become pictures of, and within, themselves.

My life as a bald boy in a hairy world

A reformed bald guy talked about discrimination, prejudice and being different . . . . My experiences with outright discrimination and prejudice are somewhat limited. My potentially most dangerous experience was with a group of very big, very angry guys who thought I was a skinhead. There were a couple of other isolated incidents, but they were not as damaging as the day the cashier who gawked at me like I was a freak from the carnival and then smiled and told me to have a good day. In fact, at least the group of guys had the decency to ask if I were a skinhead. It was the constant blizzard of seemingly tiny arrows, the stares, the faint laughter, the whispers, the acts of unwanted sympathy, that pierced the deepest. The arrows were continual reminders that I was not like everybody else. They were reminders that I was different. The whole ordeal proved to be a hair-raising experience (as the new fuzz attests to). I'll try to share what it was like to be bald in a hairy world and some of my realizations from the experience with the hope that the world will start giving all people, with all their wonderful differences, the respect and dignity that they truly deserve.

The "chemo-cut" instantly brought about people treating me differently. The stares, giggles, fear and pity seemed to be shouting, "What a freak!" or "Damn Punker" or worst of all, "Ohh, he must be another one with cancer." At times I wanted to shout back at them.

I wanted to tell them that I was nothing to be afraid of. I wanted to shout, "I'm just like everybody else. Don't treat me any differently." But one bald fact remained; people around me had hair and I had none.

The steady stream of stares eroded my self-confidence, my self-respect and my pride. I realized that much of my insecurity at the time arose from imaginary eyes and giggles; however, I had no way of discerning. It was like having a dull ache. The constant reminders, especially my reflection in the mirror, aggravated the ache more and more. I began to resent my dilemma. I only wanted to be like everybody else and treated like everybody else.

Being bald dramatically showed me I was physically "different" from everyone else. The most important thing I realized was that whether or not I had hair, I was still Spenser Somers. It took the loss of my hair and separation from others to find my individuality.

I realized that wanting to be "like everyone else" was cheating me out of being the only person I could be, MYSELF.

During the course of a two week road trip, I was in the middle of nowhere, I mean Wyoming, and I pulled off the road to a gas station. The station was closed, but there was a phone outside which I used to call home. During the conversation with my mom, two bikers pulled up. They were decked out in black t-shirts, bandannas, wallets chained to their jeans. Black leather everywhere and hair everywhere else. They looked mean. As I talked, they were staring at me, circling around the gas station. In my mind they started to appear like huge black bears circling around a campsite looking for the food pack. Well anyway, I whispered as softly as possible "Bye, Mom" and hung up the phone. I was thinking how lucky it was that

Mom didn't make me say "I love you, Ma."

One of the bears spoke, "Hey, kid, can you do us a favor?"

Full of fear, jokingly I said, "You're not going to rob me, are ya?" The two bears laughed until they had tears in their eyes, until one of them came and put his paw, I mean hand, on my shoulder and said the words that held so much truth.

"Son," he said in the soft, kind voice,"Son, don't let the costumes fool ya."

It turns out they just needed some gas so they asked if the could siphon some from my tank. In Wyoming gas stations are a rarity and the nearest one was sixty miles either way. My truck had an "anti-siphon mechanism" so our efforts were feeble. So we talked for quite a while and the bears turned out to be some of the nicest people I met the whole trip.

"Don't let the costumes fool ya." Such truth.

In order to overcome evil, temptation,
you must be humbled and well rested
in the Lord. The evil takes hold
of any hand that is not:
>   *1) in prayer*
>   *2) holding Jesus' hand*
>   *3) helping another person.*

Our five senses,
the nickel inside the
piggy-bank of my mind

I've been watching myself lately, watching in the sense of seeing how I behave towards others. It's crazy. I see myself giving and not receiving anything in return. I say that not in a selfish sense but a simple, "Well, how are you doing, Spenser?"

I'm sure you know what I'm saying. The crazy part about monitoring reactions towards others is you lose spontaneity. I seem to question impulses that generally go uninvolved. Oh, well.

I should be studying. Now, school is a joke, or wait. Is it a joke? I don't know. It's all so logical.

I've just returned from Puerto Vallarta on spring break. Experiences have a way of shaping one's character. Time molds a person as well. And in one week's time my many experiences compounded in such a short period of time seemed to have sculpted a wonderful outlook on the day-to-day ritual we refer to as life. But I must sleep for a wicked school bell rings tomorrow and my father is roaming the halls hoping his irresponsible son will keep his word about going to sleep. Tomorrow tales shall be told and memories fresh in a peaceful mind shall find a home outside my head upon paper.

* * * *

The present day's happenings seem so unimportant and lifeless, so let's travel once more to Puerto Vallarta where the sun smiles as bright as the people do below. The first few days were extremely restful — sitting in the sun all day then eating a delicious meal in town at night. Puerto Vallarta has so many secrets hidden inside poverty ridden homes, in a cab driver's dirty sedan with Jesus and the Virgin Mary's portraits to make the ride a safe one. Cobblestone streets could tell more stories than one would hear in a lifetime. The sea, a mysterious, powerful secret in itself, seems to share many characteristics of the people. Its peaceful waters and strange beauty are similar to the dark, beautiful people that solemnly walk the streets seemingly content but always wishing to reach higher better places for them and their precious children just as the sea's powerful surf wishes to grab just a little more sand with its powerful, ever grasping hands. Like the ocean knows its boundaries and accepts them so the people carry on taking what the Lord bestows upon them and holding on to their dreams deep inside the dark waters of the mind. Mexico

*has a character so strong. Nature's beauty residing with
human beauty much like a striking woman standing in a
glorious waterfall with its water falling upon her —
multiplying her charisma, yet she is still a woman who needs
food and shelter and the water needs only to follow its endless
path. And just as the girl knows she must leave and receive
her nourishment, but with food inside her and rags on her
back she knows the waterfall will always be there to take her
into paradise where she is queen, rich with nature's help.
I wish to uncover the secrets of the Mexican people, but
language barriers, my many blessings, and lack of time there
hamper my answers.*

These two giant hands
       grip my mind.
Discouragement . . .
Two hands that steal the
       color from me.
I'm left with only
       darkness.
A deep, empty darkness.
The hands' only fault is
       a solitary light, forgotten,
       over-looked.
A light that will release
       the grip and bring vivid
       happy colors back into
       focus, but first it must be found.

Staring at your face
     my gaze firm and unyielding.
The noise goes unheard.
The world passes by
     hypnotized.
Time is now no reason for
     concern.
Problems are left in the
     world.
For your smile and my heart
     gasps,
but only tears are in your eyes
     now.
And our world crumbles
     apart.
I struggle to make you
     smile, but am answered
     by streams of tears.
My heart cries with yours
     but refuses to lose the
     battle of tears.
Instead of compassion, anger
     arises.
For now I realize my
     presence brings no happiness to you.

I leave you there only
	my heart stays.
If only the heart could overcome
	the mind, we all would smile.
When your world has only
	pain, sorrow, and tears,
	look back and remember
	all of its good years.
Remember the smile you
	brought to so many
	faces.
Forget about all the bad,
	For up your sleeve, there's
	got to be some aces.

The sky,
God,
Paradise.
The smoker's lung deteriorated holes of black
breeding
        cancer that seeks revenge upon the weak
        mind that's fallen prey to a flaming drug.
Yet a face smiles.
A skin blankets the evil and the
        immobile killer's inside.
The sky blue clouds dissipated, plotting
        their revenge. Soon working themselves
        into a deluging frenzy.
        God, everywhere yet thoroughly disgusted.
        The hungry filthy beggar who lets
        his face be spat upon. Seeking
        his justice that will come soon.
        The man who spits upon him
        shall have no mouth. No tongue.
        No way of expressing his condition,
        only his ears to hear the sorrowful
        cries of others' pain.
Paradise lost — just a word — a feeling
        that lives in the mind. A light in
        the darkness only few will see.

                            • • •

Yet a face smiles.
        The eyes smile —
        Lips part.
        Teeth gleam.
        The heart cries.
The mind is free, running barefoot
        plush meadows of clover, traveling
        to unexplored lands. Solving mysteries
        words can express.
The mind poisoned by reality
        the eyes present.
The mind trapped inside a body,
        a world it can't escape.
Yet, its wings still sprout
        escaping reality — fly to
        lands of fantasy — making the
        present bearable by the dreams
        and emotions it creates through
        its soaring soul.

All the ideas, happiness and
        smiles lie in an
        undiscovered drawer that
        only needs to be open,
        revealing the contents.

Acceptance is soothing and warm, comfortable like
       faded jeans
Its only fault is it seems to take the
       motivation Hope gives.
I'm caught between giving in to the
       soft warm waters
       of acceptance or to
       take a cold shower of fighting —
The trouble with cold showers is they're
       unpleasant, to the point of painful
       and it seems you can never
       stand them very long —
And the trouble with fighting is that you can lose —
       I've lost a lot. Now it's time to smile.
       Today . . . Today — thank you for today.
May tomorrow bring the same warm smiles inside a
       dying body.

I was pleased when I saw others'
       positive and negative comments, because when
       I write, I generally write for myself
       and not for others. It's funny to
       see if they understand the poem.

In your arms again . . .

> I left your world so long ago
> traveling to a new, strange land.
> I seemed to conquer my world, fitting in
> at peace with myself. Blending
> in quite nicely.
> But the pain and suffering brought me new
> wisdom
> and love.
> A love of time and life.
> An appreciation of simple and enduring
> things.

But war always follows peace and a

> war soon began. But peace is just a
> temporary
> break from war and now war soon again.

I soon seemed lost in my superficial

> world.
> Surrounded by greed and hungry
> hearts.

I seemed trapped, not knowing

> a way out.
> But knowing that even they didn't
> know it. Crowds are made up of
> individuals, blended colors
> becoming their own color.

> > • • •

So I return to your world
    respecting it more and accepting
    it freely.
    Old love seems to blossom
    easier from freshly planted
    roots.
So this, a new chapter of a long novel
    has begun, relying on the past to
    bring a brighter future.

An ocean inside a mind

He was a dreamer. He kept his hand securely inside faded jeans. His hair covered his shiny eyes and seemed to be like long extensions of his eyelashes. A sly smile occupied his colorful lips most of the time. He had plenty to say, but his verbal thoughts traveled in circles and covered so many tangents. The listener usually became tired of riding the merry-go-round and usually got off the carnival ride with little satisfaction, only dizzy spells. Simple minds are more suited for juicy gossip served up by giggly girls than those who take an adventure upon a ride.

He had an ocean inside his mind. Tears secreted from the brown mass of hair would emerge for no particular reason. The liquid emotion flowed its river down his cheeks, passing his smile and falling quietly to the ground. His adolescent years passed quickly as they always did. He rarely laughed out loud, but softly, sometimes for no reason. It was almost a childish giggle. His thoughts were like dancers graceful and precise as a ballerina at times and as wild, uncontrolled as an Indian recklessly yearning for the rain to fall.

Some called him a recluse. He always had the many voices inside his mind to talk to. He played football as well as Jim Brown, sang better than Pavoratti, ran marathons in record time, all inside his mind. He slept little, simply the voices kept him up late at night. They never screamed or cursed rather recited poetry, whispering thoughts of sunsets, springtime and yellow flowers that with the fallen rains and baby oil became tanned beauties beneath the shiny sun.

He liked high school. The knowledge deepened the waters of his mind and gave him more years to listen to more music for his dancer to perform.

He liked the pigeons. They would graze underneath the 78th street bridge, next to his apartment. He often went there to converse with the birds. They liked him and the pieces of bread his hands would offer as tokens of goodwill. Once, right after the accident, just when the birds were going to answer where heaven was, so he could go visit his dad, two boys much older that he appeared from the other side of the bridge with air guns. The birds scattered when poorly aimed bb's clanked loudly upon one of the steel supports of the bridge. He wanted to fire his own gun at them, so he closed his eyes, found an image he'd filed back inside the negative part of his mind. Once the hands of his mind could feel the coolness of a rifle's stock, he lined up his sights and fired it. He saw one of the boy's chests explode and become a river of red blood which quickly covered his entire body. His heart had popped. Suddenly the boy's eyes sprang open. The bird killers were gone. He must not go to the bad part of the brain ever again. Killing was bad! No! He walked home, never to return to the birds. Once a grand band he'd seen four times was playing a soft tune mellowing his thoughts. The screams became soft murmurs, the dancers swayed back and forth. The waters of his mind calmed to a placid serenity. Since that day he hasn't let his mind cross the boundary to the bad part. He kept close watch to make sure his thoughts didn't wander too close. His emotion is of constant happiness. The only feelings he allowed himself.

The heart can rarely overpower
the rationality of the mind.

These voices keep me company. They fill me. They bring me happiness. But the safety they bring seems unfair. Where do they come from? I'm at the mercy of the whispers inside my mind. Why now, when I should be in Florida playing golf or bridge do they haunt me so? Whom have I angered? Why am I beating myself up? I've been at their mercy all my life. They've filled pages, kept my mind company. I've never been alone. Now it's quiet, as if they've spoken everything they care to say. They leave me alone in my old age, and I have but my lonely Cynthia to keep me company.

"I think I need a dog."

It wasn't so much the silence. I've lost my map. I'm left with only swimming in the shallow waters of my mind wanting only to dive deep into the darkness, close my eyes, and find my whispers. It is not that I'm too tired, is it? Surely not. I'm beginning to think my waters have dried up. The mermaid's whispers travel to another sea. Yes, Cynthia, it is time now to bathe in the shallow water, where the sun can be felt and the water is warm. Maybe I'm too old for diving. What has it brought me? Yes, yes, wondrous things. Now I'm left alone. People read poetry when they are lonely. Well, it is time to bathe. Let the cold and mystery be for the young.

He went inside, entering a small, simply decorated living room, wrapped a shawl, then closed his eyes tightly, as if the darkness would quiet his mind. His eyes were opened a few seconds later when the sound of his veranda door had squeakily swung open. He stared a long time out the door hoping that it would shut by itself. As he stared at the sleeping cat, the wind played with his limp hair mockingly. He felt like crying. It seemed the cold had entered his bones and had taken a tiny bit more color from his eyes.

He grabbed a pillow so tightly that his joints ached. His eyes veered from the cat to the glass door as if trying to decide who should be this pillow's victim. He finally covered his own face with the pillow. He then wrapped tightly the shawl around his body and closed his eyes tightly hoping sleep would take him before the cold.

A short time later he took the pillow off his face, staring at the ceiling. Then taking a deep breath he tried flinging the wool blanket off his body. But he was lying on it and he realized it was a foolish misuse of energy and decided to simply stand up and walk over to close the door. This too proved unfortunate, because the blanket was wrapped too tightly around his legs. For a brief moment he thought that he would never get up. He lay there a while literally wondering what his obituary would read.

"Found dead — hypothermia."

The people who said he was crazy all his life would then be the ones who were right.

One more push and the humor totally vanished and was unhappily replaced by disgust. His father's stern eyes, the look on his mother's face when he told her he was leaving home. All the faces and pairs of eyes seemed to be glaring at him shaking their heads. His high school English teacher once told him, "Artists must die a horrible death before they can be famous." Well then, death would be horrible, but fame didn't mean a whole lot for he had his cross. I have my blanket . . . found dead in living room. And around the world people would start calling the living room the dying room. That all would be o.k. If it weren't so cold. He tried once more and his left leg was freed from the would-be mummy-like snow. He took a deep breath, moved his back and another leg was liberated. He sat up, out of breath. He picked the pillow and flung it at Cynthia. He missed. He put his head in his hands and began to cry. He wanted to lie down again. If it wasn't so damn cold.

Visible darkness

No candles in the windows, for there
    are no windows.
No stars piercing the night.
No eyes to see them.
Just a spirit flowing in an empty
    darkness filled with invisible light, a light
    never seen, but totally immersed by the
    spirit. Felt, yet never seen. Crying
    without tears.
A wind blows, yet never a leaf
    quivers.

Another man's trash . . .

He was there . . .
Finally he had reached his home.
He was now complete.

He lay himself down on the cold, hard sidewalk and closed his eyes. The stench of the nearby sewer was overpowering. Slowly, the man opened his eyes, and found himself in a dew-covered meadow, lushly covered with flowers of every fragrance, size, and shape. The grass was greener than any he had ever seen before. The air, moist and sweetly scented, surrounded and seemed to engulf him. He felt as though he could drink it up, and receive new powers from the strange essence. He thought not to rise up and explore his new-found paradise, for his mind was content and realized logic was only tricking one's self into believing something. The man's mind had finally relinquished control over his senses. Senses that before were slaves to the mind, but now only served themselves.

The man looked down and saw he was sitting in a stream. He was sitting in it, but no water was touching him. Instead, the water was flowing over his legs, leaving inches of air between him and his legs. As the water flowed it changed shapes and seemed to smile at the man as it passed by him on its never-ending journey onward. The man realized that water was, and always had been, a vital and dear friend.

The beauty and mystery of the unknown place fully captivated and overcame the man. He knew now his struggles and hardships of his past life were over and a new life in paradise would now be beginning.

Strange animals now raced in front of the man. They came in all shapes, forms, and colors. All of them had black circular legs, some having more than others. Their eyes were very bright and seemed to illuminate the man's world. They stopped in unison and then proceeded on their way. Occasionally, they made a low-pitched noise that sounded quite negative. Their speed and grace astounded the man. The things paid no attention to the man, but the man didn't seem to trust the unknown creatures. They vaguely reminded the man of cars in his old polluted world.

The man, hearing a faint sound, turned his head. He stared in great awe for lying next to him was an object more beautiful than anything he had ever seen. Light bounced off the object and instantly became a spectrum, whereas the object was completely surrounded by rainbows. As the man studied the object he became aware that the object was whispering unknown words in a magic, captivating tone. The man could resist no more; he touched the object. Instantly a wave of warmth passed through his entire body. The man had never felt such contentment, pleasure, or happiness in his life. He scooped up the object and lay himself down to rest, realizing that he had found complete fulfillment and possessed all the power in his world.

It was a cold stormy night as Lou walked to his car. He had stayed later than usual at the factory, hoping to get that promotion. He was unaccustomed to walking the crime-ridden streets this late at night, but proceeded on with caution. He turned the corner on 53rd Street and saw a man lying in the sewer. His dirt-infested clothes and body were drenched from the polluted water. Lou was aware that the man must be very cold and hungry, but the fact that the lazy, old bum was loitering his highly taxed streets annoyed him greatly. Something about the bum made him feel uneasy. He took a few hurried steps past the lump. He hadn't gone far when he stole one more quick glance back at the wretched stranger. Taking another step before his glance registered, he instantly stopped, not wanting to look back. Fearful curiosity overcame the man, for in the motionless bum's hand Lou had seen something glowing. Heart pounding, he now turned and took two fearful steps toward the body. A wave of relief quickly flowed through the man, as he neared the mass he realized in the man's hand was only a bright shiny bottle cap that must have caught the light just right. He pulled his coat tight around him and scurried home, hoping his wife had kept dinner warm.

Cowboy boots are for Sunday's Sabbath
So are collared shirts.
Tucking shirt into jeans only wrinkles
them and clocks only tell when I'm
late.
Tying my shoes only takes my eyes
from the sky.
So I run barefoot.
But where?

      To run

      Running to rest, upon the Sabbath.

I bought a book of poetry.
>The poem talked of death
>so I turned the page to
>see a child being molested,
>so I closed the book of
>poetry and looked up at
>the sky.
>Turning up Mozart
>Watching the speakers quake
>with emotion.

I look at the book of poems
>opening it again. I slip through
>the poems and end up waltzing
>through biographies.
>Most of them teach.

Walking through bookstores
>skimming over self-improvement
>stopping to peek into a photography
>book. (Sunsets aren't nearly as exciting
>as boobs.)

Stumbling through poetry I feel
>the leaves of grass. But
>buy a book of selected
>Minnesota poems.

Juices eternal

I'm tired
        like a used tea bag my
        juices are bland.
        My body feels seventy-two years old.
My mind is stirring, a car in neutral, rolling
        along on its own power.
No juices are needed to listen to the wind
        sneezing rain and whipping with the
        help of clouds so high, once white
        now grey with usage.
Tired bodies sit. Resting during a
        performance of rain falling down.
Rain will never be gone, for one
        sky is but a vast lake waiting
        to dance on flower petals and
        run down the back of a slippery
        mallard.
Juices eternal.

She smiles a thousand smiles
She cries tears of rain when
        the sky's blue purity is stained
        with the darkness of foreboding
        storm clouds.
Her heart open, vulnerable.
Her soul intensified by
        emotions that flow freely.
She smiles a thousand smiles
Cries a thousand tears. Every day.
        Every day a passionate
        experience of life.
She rarely walks the path of
        life. She runs, picking the
        flowers in random bouquets,
        holding them to her chest,
        becoming a flower,
        rather than merely stopping
        and smelling them.
        Her eyes search souls for
        the priorities of life that
        one has found.

Red or is it orange? Check the eyebrows. No check the old orange neon. Red like thick blood out in the open, not inside of a syringe. Red. Period. Red. Big Red. Kiss a little longer. Red like after you're finished with a book. Red, I wonder what a blind man thinks of red. The tree warmth of a sunset resting in flowers. Red of nature. Primary color red only is only a color. The red pen of my English teacher. Her evil cursive making her ideas mine. Pounding them into my head with logical textbooks. Logic. Red is illogical, irrational. It's eye-catching. The spoon on Betty Crocker Best. Red like Lesley, no she's orange, orange like freckles, footprints of where the red sun has danced upon her face. Lobster like my dad's tan. Fine, warmth.

Days blending together like people
        on a crowded street.
Air conditioning is certainly
        God's breath after gargling with Scope.
Even blended
        colors become
        one, as mixing
        yellow to red
        makes orange.
Who am I?
I am many colors,
changing constantly,
black precedes blue
or blue precedes black.
White covers me, but brown
sometimes covers white.
Orange and yellow visit
me often, only to be chased
away by black.
Colors keep me company, but
you can hear my occasional
anger.

Don't waste time thinking
        about what could
        have been.
Concentrate on what's
        been accomplished.

God is a necessity,
not a luxury

Hmm . . . I'm starting to write again. (Both this . . . whatever . . . and in my mind.) Stories and poems. For a long time I hadn't been writing fiction. I saw it as running from truth since it was "not real." But if a story or poem makes one person glad to be alive, then it is worth it.

Since I've written, my search for God has taken many turns. On the 15th, I went to a prayer meeting. Attending it was a birthday party for Jesus. Pam who is the most spiritual person I've ever met led singing, prayers and such. The room was filled with goodness. It was powerful. I was prayed over by Pam and Lee. As they lay their hands on me and started praying, I became overflowing with a sense of calm and warmth. Warmth to the point of sweat. The holy spirit's power was felt. It is such a genuine truth, filled, loving feeling. I felt so relaxed. I became giddy. Extremely powerful. God's love powerful.

I've discovered that the feeling is quickly gone and it is full-time commitment to God and prayer that enables the feelings of lovely power to be revealed.

People ask if there is a God. Yes, there is and all we

have to do is cut through the noise, distractions and tiredness, and pray and meditate. Reach inside us to the point of feeling with God. Jesus gave us the opportunity to be on the same level as God.

It is a tiresome commitment, and it is harder now for me since I feel I know how to reach God. After I act with indifference towards him. Not taking the time, energy to give to reach the point of being with God.

I think I am healed. I think so—but it is so hard to believe. Maybe I'm afraid of committing and telling people "I'm healed." I know God will heal me, because he has the opportunity to make me as God. I keep my prayer cloth with me all the time. It is a wonderful reminder to acknowledge God in my everyday life.

I am happy to follow
Jesus' footprints, because
I know where they ultimately
lead. But I did not know
how lonely it would be to
walk alone through stretches
of wonderment.
Thanking God for the beauty
along the path, and wondering
if my praise is loud enough.

For so long I thought
the Christian life was
for weak minds and
spirits. They lacked no
adventure or excitement.
Now I daily must call
upon my strength and
the Spirit's powers to
live my daily adventure
with goodness. I realize I
have been weak by not sharing
       Jesus.
I think man is naturally
evil and he goes against
nature to reach goodness.
His grasp for goodness
is satisfied rarely
and only for a short time.

There was bright illumination in the beginning. The people fell out of favor and there was darkness. Then as a promise of the glory to come, the Lord gave the moon to the dark sky. The moon was God's covenant to the people and sure enough God gave him his sun.

But some people grew not to like the sun. There was total darkness; even the moon was gone for three days. On the third day the sun rose again in all its glory. Then people began to see it as a wonderfully powerful gift of life. People preached of the sun's warmth and people happily always felt the warmth and worshipped and prayed to have their spirit shine like the sun. Some prayed and asked for forgiveness for their sins because even though they were still sinful God had given his sun to shine before the world and light up the world with his love for them.

But some people felt unworthy and said, "Geez, God really does love us and Geez, us? Sinful us?" And so the people started to call the sun Geez-us.

June 25, 1990

Dear Lord,

Remember when I used to run track in Kansas?
How nervous I would get before the race? I hate that
feeling. But I ran, unless I got disqualified like at State.
I was so nervous, I jumped the gun. I would run and
win (or close to it, as you know). But the feeling of
victory never overcame the nervousness. Like the
graduation speech, Lord, never have I worried so long.
I didn't sleep or eat well because I was so nervous; yet
it all turned out well. I've said it's almost not worth it
because of all the attention. Remember when I'd make
a basket at a basketball game and not look anywhere
except to the ground. Lord, you've given me gifts of
greatness, Lord, and I've tried to run from them
because the nervousness before the race was more
powerful than the victory. For a long time, I haven't
been running the race for victory, especially for
your victory and glory. I've been running away from
greatness and glory instead of towards it. I'm sorry,
Lord.

The fear devours my mind and my self-
confidence. Lord, I have learned to like myself and at
times I love myself as all us selfish people do. But I
spent a lot of time not liking myself. I've always seen
myself as quite a coward. Because it seems that I was
running away from what I was supposed to be running
toward.

Forgive, Lord. Forgive me for running cowardly
behavior seeking the company of other people
running scared. Forgive me for not facing up to the
challenge. Forgive me for the beer, the pot, the sex.
Forgive me for turning the radio up, for all the weak
prayers and promises, dear Lord. You know, Lord.

Forgive me for my pride, Lord. You've granted
me with much wisdom. Help me never to use that
against you or your truths.

Dear Lord, I know I could never fool you. But I have fooled a lot of people with sweet smiles and laughter when my heart is as stained and polluted, full of muck and full of fear, full of empty promises and half truths.

Dear Lord, help me lose my pride. Baptize me, Lord. For sometimes my mind attacks me full force and my head feels like it's going to close in and my heart and spirit evaporate. I'm left numb, ready to vomit. I'm prepared to run your race, so I cower back into the bleachers to be a spectator. I've failed in so many ways, Lord Jesus.

I've fooled a lot of people, dear Lord. I never could fool myself or, of course, your holiness and purity. I'm starving, Lord, scared shitless. I know I'm supposed to run, and I know I will. Yes, because I've been trying to run alone.

Forgive me, Jesus. I read how valiant you ran. Oh, how I need your teachings. I ask you now to be my teacher, to help me. I've known that you have been waiting so patiently for me to come to you in humility. I think I've tried to come to you out of pride, and I know that I wasn't actually coming to know all, but relishing that you have chosen me. Well, Lord, teach me. My life is yours. Tell me where to run, Lord. Yes, I know I must first walk. Oh, how I long for your spirit's breeze to make my hair stand on end.

Lord, help me to love myself. Help me to love others. Lord, I must start going after the glory, seeking your smile. I go now knowing I'm not alone. I go with the best teacher, Jesus, and the best-read book, the Bible.

I trust you Lord. It's myself I don't trust. I don't trust my mind, full of its terrorizing fears that defeat me so completely, rendering me defenseless and paralyzed. The devil has beaten the crap out of me a lot. But now I invite your spirit with all its power to form my entire body.

Help me, Lord, to hold your hand to rid myself of fear and nervousness. The victory has been won! Thank you, Jesus, but as I'm a product of the harvest so as I now go out into the fields, arm me with your armor of faith and let the sword of the spirit be my help.

Dear Lord, let me proselytize for you. Let me see visions and heal people. Fill me with the power, the power of love. The power of goodness triumphantly defeating all that is evil. Fill me with righteousness, the righteousness of your spirit of your kingdom.

Just as faith without works is dead, so my lessons are not truly what I know to be true.

And praise and glory be to the Lord God, the Father Almighty, and as my Savior and Lord Jesus Christ Almighty.

February 20, 1990
Leaving for Germany
My pilgrimage begins. It's 9:15 a.m. Just finishing
packing. Need stronger faith. Healing I seek to totally expand
my spirituality. Need patience with Mom. She is frazzled.
I woke up feeling like crap. I prayed that I might feel really
nice. All praises be to the all powerful life-giving force.
The Almighty Father who lives and breathes inside of me.
Time to get going.

Late Sunday March 3, 1990
Medjugorje, Yugoslavia
It is my second night here. It is cold. The spirit is
filling me with goodness. I've handed my life to Jesus. I now
shout praises to him who has set me free! So many thoughts
fly through my head in prayer. My most beautiful thoughts,
my most powerful emotions will never be read or heard or
experienced by anyone except the most powerful one of all.
It is lonely in a way, like having a wonderful recipe of a meal
and not being about to share the meal with anyone. You can
share the recipe, but the ingredients others put together make
an entirely different delicacy. Everyone, however, seems
satisfied, at least for a time. Now that my spirit has eaten the
"bread of life," it only wants that. I've been starving too long.
Yes, ask the spirit to come and it will. Things are being
revealed. I'm afraid that the lessons of my life and whispering
of the spirit will be lost. I see how much easier it is to starve
myself. I'm afraid the whisperings will become silent. Each
new day I must rededicate myself to commitment. I must eat
even when I'm not hungry. Strength from the spirit is
achieved by hard work and manifestation of the goodness
inside my spirit. I'm learning. I have not written sooner

*because every day my soul becomes clearer, my spirit fuller, eyes
are drawn to the sky. I give thanks, for my life is giving to the
continued growth of the spirit, the cleansing of the soul, the
singing of praises of the grace and power of God's goodness.
I have much to learn. So much to experience, so much to
challenge.*

*Give thanks in life. Life is not meant to be full of
burdens, worries, and sins. It is meant to be at peace with
oneself, one's fellow man and about all people with God the
Father, the blessed sacrifice of Jesus, the image of righteousness
of all. Yes, sin stands in the way. Yes, I keep praying this is
the holy spirit taking the evil of the stainer of men. But I've
been reading the Bible, and it's clear the Son of God has
saved the world. We must accept his goodness. Let his sacred,
holy, goodness seep into our polluted stream of life and make
us clean. Once we truly repent and begin our journey toward
righteousness, then we can peer into the waters of our spirit
and see, and drink from, and be cleansed by the holy spirit.
Yes, goodness has overcome all! We must start letting God
love us. Why do we run from the only things that can give
us true peace. I must pray! I must continue to pray to free
myself. Healing has become totally secondary, but it will
happen. It is God's will. I willed be healed. Yes, Jesus wants
me whole, and I must continue to receive him and continue
to reach as far as I possibly can to touch the edge of his cloak.
Yes, I'm waiting to be healed. It will come. I trust in God's
love and in him all things are possible and total peace is
given.*

*My spiritual voice is growing louder each day. But as
the sun rises I must learn to speak anew.*

The Christian Churches today seem to
        have forgotten that Christ was dead
        for only 3 days. And that was over
        2000 years ago. We need more
        concentration on victory, his
        teachings, humility, THE POWER
        AND PRESENCE OF THE HOLY
        SPIRIT.

Fear God, yes
but enjoy the warmth of righteousness.

Filling myself — refueling
The excitement is like anticipating
        an afternoon of sitting, waiting
        for a thunderstorm humbly to begin —
RECEIVING THE SPIRIT — ASK AND
        YOU WILL RECEIVE.

Life should be giving thanks
        and praising and serving our
Lord. Everything else should
        be looked at as a distraction.

Water

There is a lake in town. It's the most beautiful, most pure lake I've ever seen. Everybody in town says so. We townsfolk call ourselves lucky to have such a great lake. Even though we didn't do anything to get it, and none of us deserves it, it's here. Some folks tell everybody all they can about it. They hand out travel brochures, maps, and even give them sunscreen. Others, they kinda' keep it to themselves. Some folks come from miles around to swim and drink and just plain gawk at the water's glory. There's always somebody getting healed of somethin' or another in the lake. Shoot, even the demons jump out of people after they see the lake. Filthy people come and get so clean that they squeak. No matter how much dirt and filth goes into the water, it remains so pure you can see your shiny clean face in it. Yep, this lake is something to behold.

The whole town loves the lake. At least that's what they tell ya'. A long way back people loved swimmin' and carrying on so much in the lake's pure waters that they formed a swim club. Today there are a whole bunch of swim clubs in town. They meet every Sunday in various places around town. They still claim to love the waters, but not much swimming goes on. Instead people bring their picnic baskets and sit beside the lake and have a nice time without getting wet. Some folks ain't never even swam in the lake before. They've never felt the refreshment or tasted the sweetness of waters. They sure are missing out. I guess that's okay, ain't nothing wrong with it, except the fact the sun sure can be hot sometimes. That's the reason for the lake I reckon', to give us relief from the darn sun. But generally various clubs that don't do much swimming cover themselves nicely from that heat.

One club, the oldest group of organized swimmers, I just don't understand. Shoot, you should see their life guards. They're all decked out with heavy white robes and gold jewelry. All that stuff protects them pretty good from that blazing sun, but everybody knows that to go swimming you've got to be as near enough to buff as decency allows. Those robes and gold seem to weigh them down. If they went swimming with their outfits on, they'd probably sink. All that fancy stuff doesn't help get somebody out of one of them swamps they have in other towns either.

This swim club has built huge buildings to shade them from that burning sun. They are spectacular structures. Some people use them as a place to change into their swim suits before barging into the lake. But most of them, after hearing the life guard tell them how unworthy they are to swim and how badly people get burned by that sun, don't feel like doing anything except putting more sunscreen on.

I guess the most disturbing thing about this swim club is that they put a lot of emphasis on the cloud that the rain fell from to form the lake. It sounds silly making the cloud seem almost as important as the lake, but they do. They have pictures and statues of the cloud everywhere.

All of them seem kinda' sad. It's like nobody has ever told them that they need to do nothing special to be a swimmer, except dive in. Now don't get me wrong, this club has produced some excellent top-notch swimmers. It just strikes me funny that the most disciplined swim club seems scared to jump into the refreshing waters and really have some fun.

Luke 2:6-6
For unto us a child is born

J esus, the Son of God and Savior of the world, soon after entering the world, was placed in a lowly manger! It doesn't seem fitting for the future King of the universe to be outside in a stable. Jesus' humble beginnings make His future greatness that much more incredible! The son of a carpenter, born in a stable, now proudly, in all His glory, sits at the right hand of God the Father.

As Christians, this lifetime is our "manger" of sorts. Life sometimes is lonely, and we may feel left out in the cold. It is important to remember this present reality is temporary. Wondrous things wait for us in heaven! Our future, like baby Jesus, is filled with promise and glory.

And like Jesus, our "Manger" is hardly unbearable. Those same stars and singing angels are for us to enjoy. Just as Jesus was "wrapped in swaddling clothes," we, too, are kept warm by the Spirit of God within us and the love of others. Whenever we are feeling alone or left out in the cold, we must remember Jesus. His warmth is only a prayer away and a very warm, cozy, eternity is awaiting us.

Dear Lord Jesus, our hearts are warm, wrapped in the fullness of Your great love. We thank you for coming as a babe to be our Savior. We look forward to an eternity spent in Your glory. In Your name we pray.

Amen.

It was getting late and GOD was obviously still hungry after dinner. He was preparing an ice cream sundae extravaganza on the horizon. At the bottom of the creation were strips of milk chocolate and a few crushed almonds. The dark shades of chocolate forming the soft slope of a woman's hip were given depth by the lighter nuts. The blazing orange sphere in all its glory atop the light chocolate was so round and perfect its pride was reminiscent of the first wheel. Airy, white whipped cream was placed above the sherbet without causing it to lose any of its proud roundness. The whipped cream looked like a social gathering of cotton balls that at any time might float away. GOD, realizing the restlessness of his puffy delight and feeling the pangs of pleasure that would soon be satisfied, started pouring the hot fudge. Slowly, oh so slowly, it began its journey to cover the treat. As the orange sphere awaited its covering, it soon lost its shape and grandeur as it started melting. It oozed into the milk chocolate, causing the chocolate to glow and it seemed the woman was donning a pair of orange spandex. The hot fudge's quest was fulfilled as the horizon and the sundae were ultimately covered with sweet, delicious darkness.

End of June, 1990

To: Brother Sam
       Dartmouth

Word up homey

Happy birthday to you, happy birthday to you
Happy birthday dear Sammy. Happy birthday to you!

Sorry the song and the letter and the gift are late, but I figured you'd probably be too hung over to read a letter anyway. In actuality, however, I've been quite lazy concerning getting you off your birthday bonanza, as well as a general summertime attitude that has been hampering (and enhancing) all activities.

I got my hair cut. That has been my major (worldly materialistic) accomplishment. I am still jobless, yet now feel no guilt and thus will remain so all summer (possibly life). Jobless as well as guiltless that is.

It's been really hot here. The humidity makes my hair curly and the air too heavy to do much. I've been mostly praying and reading.

Mom has been going to school all this week. She really enjoys it. She is at college from 7:30 to 5:00. She comes home tired but very excited and alive. It's so funny to see her, Sam. She is being challenged for the first time in quite awhile and thoroughly enjoys it. She hasn't bitched all week.

Sage is in the BWCA, has been all week. So I've had the house all week long to myself. Just Ruffer and me hanging out. Reading mainly. I thought about writing you earlier in the week, but besides the above, didn't have anything else to say. I had things to tell Sam the brother, but not a whole lot to tell Sam, the seeker of truth, enlightenment, and God.

Until Wednesday night that is.

So much has fallen into place as well as by the wayside.

When you think you (people in general . . . especially the Somers brothers) know it all, that is the greatest testament, a dark stain, revealing that you have so much to learn.

When one accepts he is a fool, then he can finally learn something. That is the first true lesson. The only truths in life are all spiritual. Jesus' words "the flesh accounts for nothing." I think, brother Sam, I thought I had this life stuff figured out. But I had the "flesh" truths down and not the spiritual truths. The same flesh truth that has brought you to the Ecclesiastic view that all is meaningless, the flesh truths that you've reached mean nothing.

And as long as you disregard God and genuine prayer/communion with God instead of meditating on yourself, this is as far as you will ever get. As long as you disregard the power of God's grace, then you will always stay upon your philosophical plateau of chasing meaningless truths that linger in the high lands. No, the truths are not in the mountains, rather they are to be found right under your nose. The trick is that you have to be on your knees before the Lord, face and nose in the dust, before you'll ever find them. We fool ourselves climbing to find truth when we should be bowing down. When we climb, philosophize and rationalize, we climb further away from where we should be, and that is to realize we can't do it on our own — that we need Grace.

Nothing is as it seems. The truest strength comes in weakness. True understanding comes only when we admit that we are fools. To serve is better than to be served. The greatest of pleasures, and greatest temptations eat us instead of satisfy. We are complete in weakness, totally whole in humility. The only time we are satisfied is when we fast, abstain. Preachers . . . arguments . . . the louder people scream the less we hear.

It's all about overcoming . . . overcoming yourself. Overcoming greed, lust, self-love, anger and our oh-so myopic view of a tiny soul. To be able to thank God for everything. It's about forgiveness, the ability to rise above ourself. And when we rise above ourself, we find ourselves in a very peculiar position, at the same level as everybody else.

I'm finally learning things, Sam. Finally listening to people. And the greatest thing is that its all been figured out.

The irony is beautiful. It takes our whole lifetime to learn to live. Once we figure it out, this life stuff, once we learn how to like life, then it doesn't matter if we are alive or not.

I feel compelled to write because I'm seeing things clearly for the first time. I'm learning I've been a fool all my life. Even a couple weeks ago I thought I had all the answers, but then I realized that I knew nothing of wisdom. I knew nothing of truth. I knew nothing about life because I knew nothing of humility.

The good part about all this is that I do not need to expand some essay or book to change lives. Truth, my friend, is already written. It's called the Bible. It contains the wisdom of the ages. Funny eh? Well, it takes a wise man to see that. And a wise man, as I already said, must declare he is a fool before he can achieve any wisdom at all. Anyone who scoffs at the fact that the Bible is the wisdom of the ages is self-proclaiming his lack of wisdom, his/her foolishness. Why? Because they have not learned the first step towards truth, humility.

Thinking one is above the Bible, or that the Jesus stuff is a bunch of religious nonsense, or thinking that the churched are somehow stupid or that they are a bunch of fools, is testament to the unbeliever's lack of true wisdom, a lack of genuine truth. When one realizes that the Bible is the Book containing all the wisdom of the ages, we'll then see the wisdom in the simpleness. Until you come to the cross as a child on his first day of kindergarten, and as long as you try to figure this life stuff out on your own, you are a fool.

The Holy Spirit teaches spiritual truths, truths that transcend all understanding. Things that make so much sense logically that we accept as truth hamper true knowledge. Let God be God. Our duty is to serve the Master and to serve others.

Grace. Funny word that I'm learning about. Funny feeling I've been experiencing for the first time as of late. To deny grace is to belittle the cross. To not bend a knee before God is a testament to your own selfishness. And selfishness coming in the form of our pride is the complete opposite of holiness or being like God.

Sounds funny, eh? But it's all funny.

The Bible is the Book of the wisdom of the ages. Funny? Joke's on you. Humility . . . You are being blinded as I was by my own pride, my own self. There is so much strength in weakness. When you are on your knees there isn't far to fall. I've learned my first lesson in life, Sam — humility. Losing of one's self. Submitting to

God. Coming before him as what we truly are, at least what I was, and am, a scared little kid.

Sam, after I had surgery for the first time, we met with the doctors for the first time. I had no idea that they were going to tell me I had cancer or that I would have to go through chemo. But that was exactly the bombshell that they dropped. The doctor from the University played the "bad cop" and, with the bluntness of a baseball bat, informed me more or less that I was in for hell. I had it in my mind that I'd end up as a bald dead guy real soon. Well, anyway, it scared the absolute shit out of me. I started to cry. I remember I cried so hard that finally I pulled the blue hospital blanket over my head. I covered my face and sobbed. Dr. Singher came in and played the "good cop," and after I had cried for a long time I finally uncovered my head and face. I think at that point I remember thinking, "Okay now, let's do what we have to do." At that point I promised myself that I would not ever cry again. And I don't think I ever did. After every relapse I would go up to my room, I would shed a couple of tears or cry for a little, but I never had let that scared little kid under the blanket show his face. Instead, I held it all inside. People calling me strong and respectable, but me inside knowing that so much of it was acting, keeping face. I was inwardly despising myself for my weakness, my fear. Always trying to forget that I had cancer.

Well anyway, last Sunday I went to this charismatic healing meeting by myself. Lee was the leader; he preached; rather, he talked wisely. We had communion and then there was a healing service. Well, last time Lee and Pam prayed over me they smoked me with the Holy Spirit. I'm talking a river, a giddy enlightenment passing through the body.

Supernatural, yet oh so natural. Anyway, I got prayed over and didn't feel a whole lot except humiliation. I guess for the first time I realized that I had cancer, would probably die real soon and I needed healing. I say realize, but like all this that I'm trying to explain, is unexplainable. Unexplainable because it is so far from the rational prison of my mind. It is freer, but even more than that, it is more real. Oh, so much more real. Well anyway, I came home from the meeting feeling really hurt and humiliated, not because I didn't get healed, rather, because I had cancer. I felt like a little kid under a blue hospital blanket, and I hated the feeling. I was scared. I felt like crying. And like most kids when they are about to cry, scared and feeling hurt, they become silent. So for a day or two I purposely did not pray. In fact, I was quite cynical towards God. Remember how Mom and Dad would come up to our rooms after we were sad or mad at them. Well, I guess that's what I was waiting for; like so many people, waiting for God to come to them. Well, he already came once and I don't think he's up to a sequel. Well, before a sermon appears I'll get on with it. I was sitting in my bathroom looking at myself and my lump (I'm still trying to figure out a name for the bugger), and I started to pray and instantly I started to cry. I cried hard, sobbed for a long, long time. It was my first full-fledged crumple up your face, full body convulse, tears everywhere, since the doctors diagnosed me five years ago. Oh, I cried hard after seeing "Beaches," but I had been drinking and I thought the dumb movie was supposed to be a comedy.

Now true lessons can be learned without thinking you are above it all, Sam. I came to realize the truth. My first step. I've been a fool for so long.

Thinking I had solved this life stuff. Pretending, hearing people tell me I have the answers yet not yourself. Sam, the blessing of intellect so easily transforms into a curse. Having to have things make sense and putting things in the place we put things where we think they should go. Who are we to judge? The more you learn the less you know — egocentricity and other prides stand in the way of everything. All we have is our life's experiences, but the more experience we have, the more cultures we see, the more time to believe, especially in God. But God is more than scriptures could ever reveal. He is inborn — He is our soul — our life force — the life force around us — the giver of life and death.

When one trusts in his own self for salvation, he walks to the gates of hell. Lose yourself and you finally have found something. Total surrender to God and finally you are strong. When we trust in our own selves, we will surely fall into the pit of hell. The strength comes only in weakness. Do not take the most important seat at a banquet. Become like a child to know the Kingdom of God. Blessed are the poor in spirit for theirs is the Kingdom of God. To be saved you must deny yourself, pick your cross and follow Jesus. When you pray, go to your room, lock the door and get on your knees. If you look in the mirror, and if you spend more time each day looking in the mirror than praying, you are in trouble. Life is a lie and we must find the truth before death finds us. The Lord gave us hands so that we might reach for him.

Dear Sam, I've gone on long enough . . . .
I love you.
Spens

In the beginning the world was filled with only light.
>>There was no darkness.
>>And it was good. The darkness entered
>>the world polluting the purity. God gave the
>>world the moon as a covenant of the
>>coming light to
>>shine and illuminate the world once again.
>>Then
>>again light came into the world.
>>It came in the form of the sun.
>>For it is written: God so loved the
>>world he gave his only begotten sun to
>>be the light of the world. For man
>>loved the darkness because of his evil deeds . . .

The more time I spend with God,
>>the more love I have to give to others.
The more love I give to others,
>>the more I receive.
The more love I receive, the more time
>>I want to spend together with
>>people to love them.
The more I love people, the more
>>each one of them even "the
>>least of my brothers" begins to look
>>like Jesus.
The more people begin to look
>>like Jesus, the more I start
>>looking like the guy.

Jesus' love for humanity indeed ran so deep he gave the ultimate sacrifice, his life. Jesus (that guy sandals were named after) truly fits the definition of goodness. He set the standards of how to deal with others and revealed the meaning of purity. "Turn the other cheek" and "do unto others as you would have done to yourself," was Jesus' main philosophy. He healed the sick and fed the poor. He preached, serving others but not oneself. He was pure. He led a perfect life, a life without sin. He was tempted, but never was his heart stained. Granted, the guy was one up on the rest of us since he was the son of God, but his life and actions are examples of genuine goodness.

Silence, the best tune you could never whistle

I've been thinking a lot lately about God and how thankful I should be (especially with my family). I love them so much, but I can't remember the last time I told them.

School is going fine, but I hate it. The whole system is stupid. I strongly believe life and true knowledge cannot be found in some text book.

I bought a book called Poets Market. *It tells of thousands of places to be published, but I read it and got very psyched and then discouraged. I don't know, I hope I become a writer some day.*

I want to talk to Mrs. Rebholz again. She's probably the force behind my high goals. Besides that, I miss her.

Sam got all "A's," not even one damn "A-." He is an awesome dude, I hope the best for him.

Sage is having a terrible time with spelling and reading. I feel so sorry for her, even though I never tell her that. I think she has a learning disability, but she tries so hard she makes up for everything. She is a great kid. I love her a lot.

I've learned how to sit
       still.
I don't need to pray out loud
       anymore. The spiritual
       voice is getting louder, clearer
       each day. But each day
       I must learn again how
       to speak.
My life is happening.
My reality is sitting
       still.
And I don't gulp from
       my full cup.
I've learned how to sit.
       Now I must learn to
       make my stand.

I become
like a clover leaf
being as still as
possible, waiting in
the glory of the
early morning
for a drop of
dew to quench,
to form upon me
to satisfy my
every need and
bring me peace.

Listening to snow

"Shh! . . . Go listen to the snow fall!" It wasn't that I was in their hair, rather their living room. Whispering pleasantly, hugging me with crisp, invisible arms, the earth seemingly welcomed me.

I stood in a social gathering of snow looking at an aqua popsicle with frosty freezer-burned clouds and opened my ears as eagerly as a Christmas gift.

I selected a snowflake that was dancing a wintry waltz and waited for the band to take a break.

Then it fell

fell

fell

And landed with a loud thump upon another unique creation who then let out a tiny scream as they embraced like old friends.

That is when I heard the muffled cries beneath my feet and the wind telling me to go away.

The wind's breeze had enough coolness
       and strength to spread his
       lips into a smile. His hair rose
       half-heartedly to absorb the pleasant
       smell of the Earth's breath from
       the scalp and swim in the ocean
       of invisible power. The dark strands
       after the congregation rose to the occasion,
       settled back down in what appeared
       to be a bow. The smile
       remained. Dimples make one
       happy.
       Dimples, not only make for smiling
       faces, but pleasant thoughts as well.
       Pleasant thoughts make for light hearts
       and lighter feet. Johnny's hands left
       the security of his faded
       Levi's pockets and he began to run. Run
       is an exaggeration, of course,
       for his muscles were unaccustomed to
       such vigorous exercise.

Sacred tears

I see you leave, gracefully and
      quiet.
Your heart and mind are on fire
      but the only visible sign is
      a solemn trail of liquid flowing
      from burning eyes.
Fire seems always to bring
      water.
Without water the heat would
      forever linger, only breeding
      more flames.
So we must never waste our
      only defense.
A sad, desolate desert seems more likely
      to spark an uncontrollable inferno.
So keep a clean mind and
      heart and forever hold
      close to you your sacred
      tears.

Johnny

Johnny could play marbles
            with the best of them.
Baseball was in his blood, his
            arm, a precise gun to
            one.
He owned camouflage pants
            his father had worn
            in 'Nam.
Johnny always smiled.
When tears visited my
            eyes his arm kept my
            shoulder company.
Johnny never washed
            behind his ears.
Johnny could always
            sleep over.
Coming home before
            dark was a rarity
            for him.
Summer's boredom brought
            countless visits with him.
Johnny never cried.
Girls were his enemies.
He was clever, even devious at
            times.

                        • • •

He could beat up my
        older brother if I
        would let him.
But most of all no one, except
        me ever saw him.
He lived and breathed
        inside my world, a
        world which we shared.
I haven't seen Johnny
        for a while, but I'm
        sure he has grown
        up a bit and even
        maybe likes girls!

The numbers hung dignified, respectable from a white freshly painted door. The sun filled the corridor, a man-made springtime. The indifferent door opened, letting two flies discover more of the world . . . . It opened a little more than half way, but a trash bag stopped it from reaching its full potential. The kitchen black garbage bags with yellow handles were indulged. Others looked like gaping mouths waiting for their mother to correct them or to chew with their mouths open. Still others, maybe having indulged too much, were leaning to one side, beer cans and spaghetti cans with flies inside instead of meatballs. The smell and flies filled the air. The flies seemed happy to be in such an environment and the irony of the name housefly was apparent. Dishes were stacked in tired piles. The heavy metal frantic buzz of the fly guitars accompanied the percussion of the faucet. The music was only faintly framed to be heard from the living room. A black/white portrait of John Lennon guarded the apartment's living room. A TV with a blank screen looked as though it was resting after jogging all ways and having pulled a few muscles. An oak desk seemed oddly out of place, like a college professor teaching philosophy to kindergartners. The desk supported a plastic Minnesota Twins cup. Erasers and the tops of pen covers could be seen peering over the plastic rim, with beautiful words covering the paper like snow atop the ground. A Schmidt beer can concealed many cigarette butts concentrating upon leaving a permanent ring on the old desk. A simple chair faced the opposite way, as if mad at the desk. It stared at a bookshelf. It was only partially full. Salinger intertwined with Faulkner and the poems of Emily Dickinson were being digested by "The Human Body."

The brown carpet was stained and probably drank the alcohol that had been spilled. The couch's arm seemed reluctant to stand on all fours and with sufficient encouragement would soon rest upon the carpet. A fan, more to keep the kitchen's smell out of the living room, than for coolness, enables one to look more closely into the kitchen. The refrigerator and freezer doors were both open. They looked like tree arms outstretched and waiting for someone to help them. Pink champagne bottles were lined perfectly on a shelf too. The drawer section — the uniformity made it impossible to corner them. The glass cupboards looked like they were trying to stretch from the hinges and give the frig the hug it needed. The white freshly painted door closes shut indifferently as you leave.

Night time again

The glowing moon smiles unto the vast sea of darkness
> below.
Gentle breezes flow through sleeping streets,
>> whispering their unknown secrets to quivering
>> trees.
Crickets tell stories in unintelligible tongues.
The stars pierce the midnight blue sky like needles
>> through a pin cushion.
The deserted streets happily soak up the night air.
>> Its coolness massaging the polluted,
>> over-traveled
>> pavement.
A lone streetlight burns a hole through the serene
>> blanket
>> of darkness. A fiery reminder that day will
>> come once
>> again, bringing a temporary end to the
>> peacefulness that
>> surrounds us.

When Grandma showed it
to me
I said, "But Grandma the cup
filled all the way
up is empty."
"Oh, but it is full, you will
see.
Close your eyes
maybe that will help
you see better."
But I kept quiet
and decided, I
might as well try it.

It's awfully cold.

Wind's winter taking full advantage of
       the naked season.

Awfully cold.

Trees shake, yet remain strong.

Green chloro-filled grass hides under
       blankets of white. Waiting

Squirrels seek forgotten nutrients
       buried in hidden treasure chests.

Solemn snowflakes gather in social
       drifts.

It's awfully cold.

The earth shivers.

Sun bringing light, yet little
       warmth.

Icicles mature every day, dreading
       the coming of a new season.

The robins will sing.

Flowers will blossom.

Animals emerge.

Humans dance.

The robins will sing.

Coals will cool in fireplaces.

The robins will sing. Soon.

The snow sacrificed its solid
      form, smashing against
      the windshield and became
      liquid that wipers eradicated
      with systematic strokes.
      Music spread its warmth through
      car speakers.
      The cold's breath fogged the
      car windows.
Ice played tricks
      on the cars.
      Wheels, the screeching
      brakes its laughter.
The ditch lay, patiently
      waiting, its jaws wide
      open ready to devour and
      consume anything that fell
      victim to the ice's trickery.

Beyond still

Outside my window,
The steam from my tea massages tired eyes,
I see the Oak Tree's brittle naked branches have
Ceased yearning for a sip of the sky,
Its thirst stymied by the cold.
Standing poised, suspended,
Beyond still.
It listens.
The wind holds its breath in anticipation.
Waiting for whispers.
But the thoughts of spring are forgotten,
Covered in heavy quilts of white silence.
And for a time the Oak Tree questions his fancy
With a liquid above.
And as I drink deeply from my hot tea
I hear a rattling of limbs
As if my old friend was rejoicing
In the wonderful nothingness of unknowing.

Well journal, since you're a place to collect and sort out my life, emotions, etc., I thought I'd make a "TO DO" list. (Something completely rare, but ya' never know, maybe I'm becoming responsible!)

TO DO

1. Math tutor — call

2. Check on guitar lessons

3. Finish-up my print-outs

4. Brings disks to school — copy

5. Build a table(?)

1-5 that ain't bad!

Let us once again make
> *our magic. Place your hand*
> *upon the pen. Let your*
> *mind travel. Unleash every*
> *thing. Grab love and smiles.*
> *Touch hate, but never let*
> *it touch you. Carry love*
> *in each step you take.*
> *Dance the dance of pure*
> *joy.*

Summer,
the seemingly endless path

Thoughts of Somers
Summer 1988

o it begins. Not summer, it is half over and its incredibly relaxing routine brings a light heart and the crickets' symphony. Not love, although every day the love of life is realized with the waking of the new day. My true love for one wondrous lady isn't beginning; the love we've shown has burned in our hearts for a while; smiles and happiness kindle the flame constantly. Pain and suffering have been with me for a time. The world is still hangin' on. The stereo still emits great tunes. The day-to-day routine we refer to as life still travels, as it has for 16 glorious years, at its lazy pace. No, no incredible, earth-shattering things are beginning. Except one. That these naked pages shall be clothed with the life of Spenser Somers. Records to look back upon, for the chapters of the summer of '88 shall become a novel someday. A novel that is being written as we speak (or yell). The summer shall end, the novel shall close, but many volumes of Spenser are yet to be written. They, as it always has and always will, bring endless stories.

I feel compelled to tell my fairy tale which has begun with the closing of spring and no end is in sight. Love, pain, smiles. Yep, this tale has it all, so let us begin soon.

I t wasn't the sun that woke me, rather the bright blueness of the sky. Clouds of sleep stifled my motivation to rise. Summertime mornings — there are no such things. The sun has afternoons. The kitchen cold floor gladly moved my feet towards the refrigerator. Thoughts still misty like eating a salad and that's all for dinner. I grabbed the milk — the refrigerator breath opening my eyes wider. The Total Raisin Bran — its love nourishment of eleven vitamins and minerals waiting to nourish — was freed from its oak cabinet prison to be served daily. Milk, and cereal laid on the cabinet — looking like a couple of nervous junior high students on a date with nothing to talk about. The bowl and spoon were freed as well and joined the couple on the counter. The bowl, well, let's say that it was the movie theater for the milk. The girl relaxed, sat comfortable in her seat.

Bubb

I t was a time of toughskins, marbles, and no underwear. G.I. Joe dolls were hand-held crusaders to save the world. It was a time of baseball cards and a time when girls were invisible, tennis-playing nothings. Whiffleball games with ghost runners, their time limits the setting sun and the dinner bell. It was a time of summer. Stress was just a word and smiles a reality. Endless hours on the lake shoreline, our rear ends extensions of our tanned, muscleless arms, and our young minds dreaming of the huge northern pike which would at some moment, probably on our next cast, be polite enough to strike and become our prize.

It was a time of searching for night crawlers and ring-necked snakes with Bubb, a first true best friend, and me. The neighbors and our parents always were complaining of the overturned rocks in the backyards. It was a time to dream, jump in the rain's puddles and roll down hills with our eyes closed. It was a time of not knowing or caring about money. A time to enjoy nature's priceless pleasures. A time to giggle. A time of abusive older brothers and nagging sisters. A time of Lake Quivira, Kansas, a private world with a security guard and an intimidating gate to keep the riff-raff out and the doctors, lawyers, airplane pilots and various other well-dressed, stress-filled people happily secure inside.

Most of all it was the glorious time we all should recall with a smile, childhood. My recollection definitely brings a smile and more memories than can ever be realized on paper.

Summer '89

1. Meditate daily
2. Write twice a week
3. Guitar
4. Write
5. Don't chew
6. Write
7. Exercise
8. Eat right
9. Meditate
10. Love God, myself, Lesley
11. Love God, Lesley, myself

Sitting, bare feet absorbing freshly cut grass.
Body absorbing lawn chair
A Lawn Boy fart, indulged.
Body fat, indulged
Grass, brown spots, desert islands in a sea
        of green
Brown spots on hand, chest, eating life
        like crabgrass.

Night came wandering in
exiting off I-70 E and I
realized I was in Colorado.

Houses spotted mountainsides like
beard stubble on a hitchhiker's
face. And I realized I was
in Colorado.

I put jeans on. My favorite
faded Levi's that let my knee
caps see the storm rolling in.

Sleep felt good
And I knew
I'd stay.

They say spring's living fragrance
        brings love, and that summer's
        heat brings freedom and happiness.
Love without freedom and happiness
        is no love at all.
Our love shall never be contained
        with the closing of a season,
        or the sands of time. For the
        eternal smile inside my being
        shall warm the spirit and forever
        recall the incredible warmth of
        the summer's sun.

Summer memories linger
but school spirit soars

When I was asked to write "What I did this summer" I had a rather frightening flashback to elementary school and that grey, wide-lined paper. After a short time (a recess if you will), I was comforted by the fact that I am to be a senior in the fall. That realization was also unsettling because the answer to the question would have to consist of more than "I had fun; I went to a friend's house. I laughed." It's funny to think that those three sentences sum up this summer and every summer since third grade just perfectly. I am seventeen years old, however, and this isn't grey, wide-lined paper.

I could tell many blissful summertime tales experienced with my girlfriend, but I'm saving those stories for a future Harlequin romance novel. If I told of the wild experiences with my guy friends, there would be a lot of trouble and you probably wouldn't believe me anyway. So, to save time and respectability, I will tell a little bit about my ten-day road trip this summer. I will concentrate on my solemn drive to, and observations about, Norton, Kansas.

I was tired of driving the truck-infested interstate and decided to travel the lonely highways of western Kansas. The striking blue of the sky seemed to illuminate the soft, rolling hills. The land is so benign that people seem to have overlooked any reason to conquer it with the steel of civilization. The humble beauty of the land enters through open windows and sets your mind at ease. Pickup trucks and houses are as rarely seen as speed limit signs. To pass too quickly through the serene landscape would be like wanting a glorious sunset to hurry up and go down.

Norton, Kansas: population 2,974. It proudly bears the title of "Pheasant Capitol of the World" and is the home of the '85-'86 4A state football champs. Its laid-back style of living is reflected in the faded overalls and slower speech of the people who live there. It is a place where teenagers still drag main street and adults talk about wheat prices over coffee at the drugstore. In the restaurants, the men's restrooms are generally located before the ladies and the only place you can get fish is in a sandwich at the Dairy Queen. People wave to each other from their American-made cars and trucks. It has the closeness of one big family.

Both of my parents grew up here. They fell in love at the Lucky Strike restaurant. My mother came from a farming family of nine, so relatives abound like sunflowers on the edges of the roads. My main objective while in town was to visit as many branches as possible of the family tree.

I had a pork chop breakfast with my Uncle Loren and Aunt Greta. Loren is a pig farmer as well as the respected real estate man and auctioneer in town. I stayed with my Uncle Chuck and Aunt Beverly. Chuck owns, and, with the help of three children, operates the only bank in town. My cousin showed me the beloved ribbons he had won at the county fair. I helped chase chickens back into their coop with my cousin Karl. I visited my eighty-six-year-old grandma in the nursing home whose vigorous, loving smile could make anyone speak with a softer tone and walk with a slower stride. These things seem rather trivial, but all were experienced with a smile. It was reassuring to see

the gentleness found in these characters and to
rediscover how important family is.

I apologize for going on about what some may
see as just a small town in the middle of nowhere, but
I have discovered that the most sincere places in the
world don't have a single stoplight. Norton is the
heartland of America. And like hearts should be, it is
pure-pure American.

Summer is almost over and Kansas is just a
pleasant memory. The school bell at old EHS will soon
be heard. I'm not looking forward to paying fifty
dollars for a parking permit, waking up in the middle
of the night to go to school or having my high school
graduation inside a hockey arena; however, it will be
great to see the wonderful students and teachers who
make EHS such a great place to go to school. I think
the spirit of the class of 1990 will lead the school to
new heights.

Hair borrowed from the sun's
        heart.
Eyes chipped from the many moods
        of the sky.
Tears of the poet.
Her smile, the pierced lips, like
        a sunrise split by the horizon.
Kisses like soft summer raindrops.
A face of smooth white marble, sharp
        nose and chin.
Dimples, invisible happiness inside.

Sitting at a fountain trying to change the world

OLDMAN.   Whatcha thinking, friend?

TIMMAN.   Not thinking at all, just trying to keep thoughts from my mind.

OLDMAN.   That's what the fountains are for, I guess . . . Never seems to work though, especially here. The water's sound soothes the mind and before you know it, whatever you're not thinking about is forgotten and the relaxation of the water causes you to smile.

(Laughs)

TIMMAN.   (Turning now) You're probably right.

(Silence)

Sounds like you've been here before.

OLDMAN.   Yep.

(Silence)

I just made a run to the liquor store actually a nice walk.

(Unscrewing bottle, spitting, then sipping)

A little nip of the old spirits helps keep this old spirit going. Not too often. Don't let me lead ya' on. Just enough to help fountain's waters sound a little smoother.

TIMMAN. No thanks, I betta be going.

OLDMAN. Oh, shoot, go ahead, son, if it's that AIDS thing you're worried about, don't you worry. Not that I haven't tried to get a little action at the retirement community. But them girlies just like their soap operas and when they are not watching the TV, they are going to the chapel. Nope. I'm clean, too clean.

(Laughs)

TIMMAN. (Smiles and takes bottle)

(Small sip)

Thank you.

(Silence)

How about another?

Sure thing.

(Silence all the waters rushing)

OLDMAN. (Takes two quarters. Hands one to Timman)

It helps to make wishes in this here fountain.

(Tosses coin. Gets up to leave)

TIMMAN. Thanks again . . . I wish I could change the world.

(Tosses coin into the fountain. Smiles)

OLDMAN. So my friend, you just did make a change.

TIMMAN.	Please sit down. I'm Timman Sanderson.
OLDMAN.	Well, hello, Timman, I'm Sam. What kinda name is Timman?
	(Laughs)
	What were your parents thinking, son?
TIMMAN.	(Smiling)
	. . . My mom always liked the name Timothy and after having three girls, my dad said he didn't care what the name was as long as he got a man out of the deal. So they called me Timman.
	(Laughs)
OLDMAN.	(Produces bottle)
	Naw, Timman, once you've unscrewed the top of the whiskey a couple of times the heart seems to open up as well. I want to talk to you, Timman, but mind yourself. I don't need to have your heart spilling out cause once the heart starts a watering, and, before you know it, everybody's looking like a fool.
TIMMAN.	(Laughs, drinks deeply)
	I promise no tears.
OLDMAN.	Good. I know.
TIMMAN.	So what brings you to the fountain?
OLDMAN.	Well, that's what they're here for. I guess our hard-earned dollars are at work.
	And if we didn't work so darn hard

there probably wouldn't be any need for the relaxing waters.

TIMMAN. Cause and effect. I tell you cause and effect.

OLDMAN. (Sips bottle)

I used to come here a lot during college, looking for girls.

(Mostly laughs to himself)

See back then I felt alive, excited about my future. The dreams were as fresh as the girls' faces. You know the feeling. A time when the sky is bluer. The grass is greener, and it's easier to wake up in the morning.

(Wildly)

Boy, your body's strong and tired.

TIMMAN. No kidding, at 13, tired. I wanted to be a writer or a poet.

OLDMAN. By the look at your eyes, you still do.

TIMMAN. Sure, but now I'm stuck up at the newspaper, writing stories concerning church bake sales, small conveniently set fires, writing huge amounts of nothingness. It seems a waste of using the precious words.

OLDMAN. Well, then quit, boy. Quit! Write! Write until your hand falls off if it makes you happy.

TIMMAN. I tell myself that a hundred times a day.

OLDMAN. If it's the money you are worried about,

shoot, what's it done for you so far?
The green bill has sat around gnawing
away at your dream and pretty soon if
you don't change, the dream will be
eaten away, and all you will have is a
nice comfortable, stable existence with
nothing to get up in the morning for.

TIMMAN. Of course, you're right. I know that I've
known that from the first day I took the
job. Only back then I promised I would
write at night. Promises have a way like
leaves losing their color, falling down
and being swept away.

OLDMAN. Here, Timman, I got this theory. See it
all goes back to Adam and Eve. Think
how happy they must have been
running around naked all the time
being perfect, being perfectly happy.
I think it is a better time and then of
course the apple .... You know the story,
but this is an old man's theory.

(He takes a coin, sets it on his thumb
ready to flick it)

See the world back then was like the
water here (points), except calm,
placid. Right then Eve took the dreaded
chomp.

(The coin goes into the fountain)

Bam! Everything was changed. See the
ripples are still shaking the world.

See we don't see them, it's because
that's all we've ever known. The world
is spinning so quickly that we don't

even know that it's moving. The point
is, Timman, now there's so many ripples
going on that everything is affected.
We drive cars whose exhaust kills the
ozone which causes some old lady to
get skin cancer which causes her to die
which causes her son to turn his back
on God and so on and so on, but I tell
you, boy, as powerful as those ripples
are

(Grabs another coin)

if we make some changes we still can be
happy. With the prick of the thumb . . .
Sorry boy didn't mean to bore you
none. You understand?

TIMMAN. I think so.

(Smiling)

OLDMAN. (Tired)

Well, I'm going to go now. There's a
little shindig at the retirement home.
I promised to bring the booze.

TIMMAN. Wait. Stay. I . . . Please come back
tomorrow. I'd like to tap some more of
your fountain of knowledge.

(They both smile)

OLDMAN. Certainly.

(He parts)

ays and nights are starting to blend together making time truly external. But the happy combination brought by the summer's heat also brings the fear of the knowledge that it will be over soon.

Tonight's heat brought something else, however, a huge thunder storm. My baseball game was happily called on its account. The rain was certainly welcomed by the grass which had transformed into sharp needles under bare feet. Green was a color rarely seen this summer for rain paid few visits.

The night brought flooded streets, stalled cars and a dubious sky. The sinister black, a perfect backdrop for the contrasting lightning that seemed more like nerves racing across the spinal cord to the brain than a show of God's power. The sky was a black man whose hearty laughter would ever so often cause him to pierce his lips and expose his sparkling teeth. The crickets' talking outside has made my eyes weary and my mind lazy. I shall sleep for now.

Let the sands of time sculpt themselves into a gracious sandcastle for the soul to someday reside

"I let my music take me where my heart wants to go."

"The Wind," Cat Stevens

This quote has a lot of meaning right now, for I want my writing to take me away. I know I want to be a writer. I know I'm not going to use geometry, but why did I fail? Why can't colleges realize I can't sit down and study. I can't seem to fit the mold of a straight "A" student, for it's not even a mold but a way of life, a way of life that gets people killed at the age of 45 of a heart attack.

It's not theorems or biology that run through my mind, but stories. So why can't I just write something for the whole world to love and adore. A story or poem that makes everyone read and say, "That was hot."

I run the chance of never going anywhere for math, and frustration stands in the way of success as well as a good college.

Oh, well, wish me luck and smile!

"Trouble, oh trouble, set me free, I have seen your face and it's too much for me."

Cat Stevens

Solemn, lonely thoughts of a shitty day

The future is a mystery, present a
            nightmare, past but a memory.
Freedom ahead, smiles and beauty
            soothing laughter soon become the
            present only to be turned into
            past memories.
Reality all too soon slaps my
face, not bringing sense, but
fear, for once again the present
transforms into the past and
the circle cannot, will not
be broken.
Time......

Dad's pressure is on . . .
            I'm applying to following schools:
                        Dartmouth
                        Colorado College
                        Macalester
                        St. John's
                        Carleton
Huge ordeal. Mom helping me with typing and
organization.

January 9, 1990

Director of Admissions
DARTMOUTH COLLEGE
Hanover, N.H. 03755

Dear Director of Admissions:

Whew! Please find enclosed my application to Dartmouth. If there is anything that I left out or forgot, please let me know!

I'm really excited that I'm being considered for the Freshman class of 1990 at Dartmouth!

If this application is late, please consider that as of this week, I have completed daily radiation treatments for six weeks. Fatigue won over working on my application on certain days!

My brother, Sam, will send you a letter of recommendation as soon as he returns from traveling in China—sometime in February. I really could have used his help in applying to Dartmouth.

My mother too is working on some sort of Personal Statement in regard to my character that you should receive soon.

Thank you for your consideration. I know I would be an asset to the Class of 1994!

Sincerely,

Spenser J. Somers

Q.   If I were to change one thing about my country.

Hmmm: A mandatory naptime? No. I don't want to give the impression I'm lazy. How about an official policy making faded Levi's and cotton T-shirts the official garb of the U.S.? No, too flaky, besides Toughskins add a lot to childhood. If I were able to change one thing . . . . Well, as I look out my window and see the strength and wisdom of an old oak tree slouching under the magnitude of the sky I smile. I'm confident I am able to make a change, simply by closing my eyes and whispering:

> Dear Heavenly Father,
>> Give us peace,
>> For a moment, please.
>> Reveal for only an instant how life
>>> was intended.
>> Grant us peace.
>> And make the peace salty, Lord.
>> Like a potato chip.
>> Leave us yearning for more.
>> Make us like your flowers, waiting
>>> Amidst the glory of the early
>>> Morning for a tiny drop of
>>> Dew to satisfy our every need.
>> Give us peace. Please.
> Amen.

Q.   Which academic subject in school is most meaningful to you? Why?

My social problems class is my most meaningful subject. It has examined such national concerns as AIDS, abortion, and drugs. The class has opened my eyes in many respects, but has opened my heart in many more. It has shown me that there is not always a "right" and a "wrong" when dealing with situations. Generally, the problems deal with conflicting "right." In college I plan to explore more thoroughly the teachings of social problems and sociology.

Briefly describe any scholastic distinctions or honors you have received since tenth grade.

October 12, 1989 — Homecoming King, Edina High School

November 20, 1989 — Guest Speaker, De LaSalle High School, General Assembly (500 students)

December 14, 1989 — Rotary Guest Speaker

May 21, 1989 — Loft-Public Reading (a place for writers and writing)

One-Act Play Contest — Minnesota Region 6AA 2nd Place, *Rosencrantz and Guildenstern Are Dead*

Published in *Images on the Wind*, EHS, National award-winning literary magazine

Published in National Poetry Anthology

Please list, in order of importance, those pursuits which best represent your principle interests outside the academic classroom.

> Writing
> Church Senior Youth Groups
> Praying/Meditation
> Junior Class V.P. EHS
> *Images on the Wind* Staff
> Basketball/Baseball
> Reading

In which fields of study have you been most interested and why?

Art and Literature—By creating something or appreciating creative works I feel more connected in the positive energy of humanity. I see creating as the ultimate positive activity.

Vocational objective—To use my gifts and strengths to further manifest the goodness inside myself and others. I hope to someday work to further people's awareness of the beauty in each day. I hope to do this by working as a teacher and/or writer.

What books or authors have particularly impressed you?

The *Bible*, Salinger's *Franny and Zooey*, *Zen and the Art of Motorcycle Repair*, and Steinbeck's *Cannery Row*.

How did you spend last summer?

1. Attended classes and wrote at the Loft.
2. Traveled to Colorado and participated in a National Church Youth gathering.
3. Helped my mom, mowed the yard, chauffeured my sister, etc.
4. Grew hair.
5. Went for acupressure therapy with my Chinese doctor.
6. Received Healing Hand massages.
7. Organized a garage sale to earn money— profit $1000.00.

Briefly elaborate on the activity or activities you find most meaningful.

Praying is my most meaningful activity. It gives me the sensation of being in God's presence. The benefits of praying are phenomenal. Strength, healing, forgiveness, and counsel are just some of the many gifts praying produces. By interacting with God, it gives me a humbling sense of inner peace.

"Ask, and you will receive, that your joy may be full." John 2 16:24.

Q.   You have answered many questions on this form, all asked by someone else. If you yourself were in the position to ask a thought-provoking and revealing questions of college applicants, what would that question be? Now that you've asked the ideal question, answer it.

I had been thinking about this question that I had to ask and answer for several days. I was pleasantly frustrated by it and didn't know exactly why. As fate would have it, I ended up where a lot of people do when they lack direction — at a gas station. As a favor to my parents, I was to have the oil changed in their car. I sat there in the station surrounded by anti-freeze, batteries, and tires. With so much stuff around me to produce smooth riding (excuse the pun) a completed essay was inevitable.

My question and resulting essay was, dare I say, "jump started" by a gasoline attendant named Jeff. He (metaphorically and physically) washed my windshield and enabled me to see things more clearly. He showed me that I was limiting my thinking concerning this essay.

As I waited for the car, Jeff asked me what I was writing. I replied that I was wronging more than writing. He gave me a frustrated look and persisted. I told him that the essay was to ask any question you wanted to ask. His eyes sparkled. He smiled. He seemed transformed into a child-like state. At the time I did not understand how the essay topic could have him burning rubber and me spinning my wheels. His face took on a mystical quality. I pictured his mind exiting off the heavily traveled main interstate and journeying to the backroads where all the truly profound questions reside. I realize now his excitement stemmed from the fact that I had neglected to inform him he had to answer the question. He seemed to be searching the obscure roads for the questions. Then I mumbled, "Oh yeah, I forgot. You have to answer the question as well." His facial expression changed dramatically. The seriousness of his face revealed he had obviously slammed on the brakes, flipped a U-turn Starsky and Hutch would have been proud of, and started heading back toward that well-traveled interstate immediately. He was returning to the place that contains answers, not questions.

That's when I realized why this essay of having to ask and answer my own question was troubling me. My "headlight" flashed on high beam. I had been concentrating on the answering of the question instead of concentrating on the question. I was restricting myself to what I knew and what I could answer rationally. As I thought this over the answer to my question concerning my question was answered. I had gotten myself in a traffic — I mean terrific jam by staying on the main road. I had been limiting my thinking.

Why do we limit our thinking? Why do we cling only to what we know? We sometimes seem afraid to cross boundaries that were made by ourselves. What stops us from traveling these backroads of our mind where we have no maps to guide us? We erect many walls to protect us from the unknown. "Argue your limitations, and sure enough, they're yours." (Richard Bach)

Our thinking encounters limitations once we stop questioning. I recently heard on the radio a Nobel Prize winner commenting on why recent cancer research was not effective. He cited that researchers, before they could receive funding, had to tell Congress not only what their research would consist of, but also what the results would be. Because of financial reasons, scientific method and questions took a backseat to answers. We cannot make new discoveries when we follow the same paths all the time. We must continue to ask questions that appear not to have answers. These questions seem to be asked only by children.

Even children, however, soon are transformed into limited thinkers. Answers and logic replace the questions. Schools and teachers generally teach students how to be great imitators. Instead of learning things for themselves, they simply have to memorize other people's thoughts. They are not taught the value of questions. They are taught the value of answers. We limit ourselves in ignorance, granted, but we also limit ourselves in rational thinking. Science and rationality have made the world a very neat and tidy place. A very limited place. A place of theorems, numbers, and above all, answers. Every rational question is accompanied by a theorem, a map, to guide you safely to your destination. Anything irrational is labeled as being wrong. People become comfortable in this orderly world. It's only ideas like the wind and God and love that make people peer over their concrete (sequential) walls to see what they are missing.

Humanity traps itself in small worlds when we limit our thoughts. We seal ourselves in a microcosm when we stop questioning. It takes ideas like the wind, God, and love to make us realize the hugeness of the universe and the smallness of our thinking sometimes. We have built vast walls with rational answers. These walls protect us from the unexplainable, the irrational. It's sure hard to get a good look at the sunset, however, without climbing over the walls. We must continuously expand our minds by questioning. Once we start tearing down our walls of limited thinking, we not only start seeing more sunsets, but it also becomes apparent that there isn't anything separating humanity.

Spring 1990
Dartmouth — Accepted
Colorado College — Accepted
Macalester — Accepted
St. John's — Accepted
Carleton — Wait Listed

Where will I go?

Youth comes but once. Life is every day.

---

*H*ello again — same time/and place, different page — I've been thinking about the future a lot — college, this summer, marriage, children, death, after death, etc. It's very hard for me to think beyond today. A lot of that is fear I think. When I say "the future" I don't mean the future of my relationships. I have too much faith in them to have fear any more. I mean my future. Yeah, when I think of what tomorrow holds for me, I often become frightened. I find myself too often talking about college and in the back of my mind truly wondering if I will be alive to see my first professor. I know I'm not afraid of death. I think of dying as a peaceful beginning to a better existence. No, it's not death I fear, rather the thought of not accomplishing all that I want to. Granted, no one is ever truly accomplished, or fulfilled, but I don't want to miss my chance to give it a shot.

It's easier to touch the sky when your head is already in the clouds

August 4, 1988

*W*ell, Thursday has come once again bringing an anniversary, an anniversary of my meeting, not meeting, rather, experiencing *Lesley McBurney. She is the reason for my smiling eyes and heart. The encounter was almost three months ago and still is as fresh as a breeze after a summer shower and as comfortable as a cotton T-shirt complementing faded jeans. Loving Lesley comes so naturally. The poet's words and artist's paintings of true love bring not only new understanding, but also a common bond of the most precious thing in the world, love. Love and beautiful are surely the most over-used words in the English vocabulary; however, when it comes to McBee* *they could never be used enough.*

You shall hear more about Lesley, but all the paper and ink in the world could never be enough to give her justice. Not until her hand upon your shoulder, your heart was in her palm and hers in yours, and experiencing the lips caressing yours could you know the Lesley I care so deeply for.

Enough! I'm getting sappy, but if we were never sappy our pancakes wouldn't be too tasty. My parents and family are going to Kansas for the weekend. They've given me the pleasure and responsibility of staying by myself. A responsibility I shan't abuse. Pleasure can never be abused, and this weekend shall be quite pleasurable, I'm sure. I'm looking forward to see how it turns out.

Life is simple. Smiles and giggles help stress vacate my body. It is summer, however, and stress is but a word that lingers in schools and businesses across the nation.

I must get my rest, for the upcoming weekend will certainly be sleep-free, an attempt to make it as long as possible. After all, there's 24 hours in a day and 0 hours for the night.

Hello, my sweetest of all

Lesley, I just wanted you to
       know how much you mean
       to me.
I've been bathing in your warm
       waters of love for a long time
       now, and just wanted you to
       receive some of the precious
       liquid as well. Rarely does

• • •

a moment pass where I'm
not thinking of the wonderful
thought of Lesley. The
strength you've given me is so
real. Your walking into my life
on a 6th hour in May was a
gift that no birthday could ever
give. A gift we share every day.
It was so great to meet a real
person. A person so easy
to fall in love with.

It's all so natural, yet so
irrational. But emotion
is something you could
never find in a geometry
textbook, right? Lesley,
you've touched my life
with such a gentle hand.
You've brought happiness
few will ever experience and
I am so happy I have. Especially
with your loveliness. Fear is wiped
away by your incredible smile.

In the insane routine known as
life, you've brought sanity with a
smile from the heart.

I love you more than words could
ever convey. My soaring
spirit needs no wings, for I
have your love.

Hello, Lesley Love!

I love you.
>The words find meaning
>And I SMILE.
>The smile brings pleasant
>warm thoughts of you
>that make my eyes laugh.

I hope for the best for you.
>Hoping the sky has no
>clouds, but that my thunder
>can be felt with a sunny day.

We are free . . . again.
>free for your touch,
>maybe that's why I can feel
>your touch so surely, so sincerely.

I love you like cars thrive
>upon pavement and
>stars shine with the
>sun's reflective warmth.

Love brings smiles like a good tune
>on your car radio brings slowed speed.

And I smile with your red hair
>glowing inside the unexplored
>regions of my heart and
>faded Levi's.

>. . .

Oh . . . By the way, did I mention
       that I miss you?
       I miss you like the birds
       hate winter's motivation to
       visit Florida . . .
       The journey's long.
But the beach's warmth
       enters through whitened feet
       into thoughts like an unheard rhythm.
Soon Florida's homecoming
       shall be our own
       and I
              will touch
              your feet.

Lesley

Me and Les.
Les and Me.
Two pebbles of sand.
The sea licks us.
We enjoy the cleansing.
Some drowned.
The sun warms us.
  We bathe in the glorious light.
  Some are blinded.
Hands once throwing pebbles
  to the sea.
They recognize the beauty we
  share.
Instead of tossing us to the
  fish, they sculpt a grand
  sandcastle.
They crown us King and Queen.

Tuesday, September 20

Hell◆ (here's your diamond!) Lesley

Well, my love, it is late, a silence has overcome the Somers' hold. Alone in my room. I've had my sleep for five days. My mind racing . . . heart content. My body, well, weakness has brought other powers.

Lesley, it's hard to explain the feeling of getting out of the 5-day prison of a hospital bed. I guess I completely shut out the world and the awakening of my mind, the mind, is insanely powerful. Les, I seem to be bombarded by sound, touch and most of all emotion. Songs bring tears to the eyes. The sunshine . . . ahh smiles. And Lesley . . . try happiness. Yeah, Lesley, you are more powerful than any drug. I think you should be a drug. EXTRA STRENGTH McBee — we could make millions.

Bon Jovi sings about bad medicine — he should try chemo.

I miss you!

Love . . . a wondrous thing

August 15, 1989

Dear Lesley,

Hello, friend. How is my love? I
miss you already. Ruffer says Hello.
I long to hear your voice,
to see your smile.

How can one feel so empty?
How can one feel so alone?
The one feels so
empty, alone.
Simply become my sun.
It's miles away.
The voice-empty in
my heart.
The loneliness because you
are miles away.
Manhattan Island
But I'm not a
foreigner.
I see you daily. Yet you're
so far away.
Love — It's a definition lost
inside lonely hearts.

Hello Lesley Ann

H appy Easter — Christ has risen today. Alleluia! Yes, Happy Easter Les. Well, I'm in Sun City, Arizona and yep, it rained all day today. The rain, however, didn't keep the Somers clan from having fun. It has been great so far. Yesterday we played tennis. (I got worked by Sam and Mom.) I miss us playing tennis, especially the triumphant feeling I felt afterwards. We've played three games of Monopoly in two days! My God, remember Monopoly? It's so fun, and yes, Les, I'm giving up my ambitions to write and I'm going to concentrate on corporate raiding. Only kidding. However, I feel I can definitely relate to Mariette better through my Boardwalk(ing) experience.

It's been a totally family couple of days. Since there's nobody else around we are forced to become better acquainted with one another. I'm really enjoying just sitting around and talking and laughing with the Somers. My dad's brother Dale (my uncle) and his family are here too. I think you met them at Christmas time. Their whole family is a riot. And Sam, my God, how funny he is — as funny as an insensitive conservative, concrete sequential, cocky, collegiate can be — I assume. He really has come into his own. He seems so old. He even played bridge today with the 'rents. He's realizing how intelligent he is and (in his mind) how stupid the rest of the world is. There's nobody in the world like Samuel Clayton Somers (thank God!). It's really good to see him and be with him.

I'm extremely relaxed for the first time in a while. I think I'm usually content, but it feels great to be relaxed and content. If that makes much sense.

We have golf tomorrow and yes, Spenser is old enough to finally drive the golf cart — oh good. But I might sleep for now — thousands of stories to tell. Soon they will reach your ears/eyes.

I miss your beautifulness because I love your wonderfulness.

Even though I'm in AZ, I'll never desert you!

A shapely story

(Love comes in many shapes, forms, and smiles . . .)
So it begins . . .
It was a lovely springtime day in May.
A blue square was hurrying to work.
This blue square's name was Simon.
Simon the Square.
As he was rushing, he passed a beautiful red circle.
This beautiful red circle's name was Shirley.
Shirley the Circle.
Simon saw Shirley's wonderful roundness.
He saw her radiant redness.
He knew she was smilingly special.
However he had to go.
Shirley saw Simon as well.
It made her smile to see him.
And she did not know why.
Days went by . . .
Simon was going home after work.
He was very tired.
He saw Shirley walking through the park
rather dreamily.
She seemed so pleasant.
He said, "Hello."
She smiled and said, "Oh hello.
It certainly is a beautiful day don't you think?"
Her voice was so sweet. Her smile was so warm.
Simon's tired eyes now sparkled and his feet seemed
lighter as he stepped closer to Shirley.
He extended his hand.
"My name is Simon. Simon the Square."
"Well hello, Simon. That is a nice name.
I am Shirley. Shirley the Circle."
They shook hands.
"Would you like to walk in the park with me?
We could listen to the bird's many songs.
We could smell spring's wonderful gifts, the flowers."

Simon's smile was answer enough.
And so they began to walk through the park.
Soon Shirley said, "Take your shoes off Simon.
Feel the cool grass with your toes."
Simon was fascinated by this red circle.
He took his shoes off and began to laugh.
Simon never went barefoot.
"I feel more connected to nature
when I am barefoot," she announced.
This made Simon laugh even harder.
They walked.
They smelled springtime's gifts
of freshly bloomed flowers.
They enjoyed listening
to the songs of the just-returned-home birds.
They both were happy.
And they did not know why.
Simon remarked how nicely rounded Shirley was.
Shirley complimented Simon on his sharp edges.
All too soon Simon realized he must go home.
He had to work the next day.
They promised to meet in the park the following day.
As Simon walked home smiling,
he noticed his blue square was different somehow.
And as Shirley skipped home she noticed that
her red circle was somehow changed as well.
The next day they met as planned.
They began to walk through the park.
Soon Shirley announced,
"The sky is so very blue today."
They looked up smiling.
Then Simon spoke,
"You are a dreamer, aren't you Shirley?"
Simon asked.
"Yes, I am a dreamer. It is easier to touch
the sky when your head is in the clouds."
This caused them to laugh.
"Sometimes," she continued,
"I walk around looking up at the sky.

The clouds are so soft.
The blueness of the sky seems so welcoming.
The sky is like a warm lake to swim in.
Are you a dreamer Simon?"
"I am not a dreamer.
I think dreams are the futile hope
that the sun will shine brighter tomorrow."
After he spoke he crossed his arms over his chest.
"No, Simon. I don't think you understand.
Hope is never futile, and the sun is bright enough!
Look up at the sun, Simon."
He looked up at the sun.
He replied, "The sun is too bright. I cannot look at it."
"If the sun is so very bright,
why would anyone want it to be brighter?" Shirley said.
"Hmmm . . . ," He said.
He had never thought of it that way before.
"Maybe you are correct, Shirley."
And then their eyes met.
They had to turn away from each other.
Their eyes, like the sun, were too bright to look into.
It came time to say good-bye once again.
As Simon lay in bed that night he realized
his bright blue was changing color.
He also realized his sharp edges were becoming softer.
He did not know why.
The next day they met again in the park.
The birds were filling the air with song.
The flowers were filling the air with fresh fragrances.
The sun was filling the air with warmth.
The air was full.
Simon and Shirley
were talking and laughing as they walked.
Then Simon asked,
"Is it hard to be a dreamer, Shirley?"
"Hmmm . . . ," said Shirley,
"Well sometimes it is.
Sometimes I'm so busy looking up at the sky
that I don't pay attention to anything else.

Sometimes I fall on a rock or something
because I'm not looking where I'm going.
And sometimes people stick their feet out and trip me.
Can you believe that?"
"The world is hard on dreamers," he said.
Then they were sad
because the world is hard on dreamers.
Suddenly Simon said,
"I know a way you can dream
and not be troubled by un-dreamers."
"How Simon, how?" she asked.
"Well it's quite simple.
First, you must learn
when it is a good time to dream and when it is not.
It is not good to walk around dreaming
and not looking where you are going.
You could hurt yourself, or hurt others.
So Shirley, when you want to dream simply sit down.
Then look up at the sky and dream.
That way you will not hurt yourself or others!"
"Oh Simon that is wonderful!" she said.
She was so excited she stopped walking and sat.
She looked up at the sky and started to dream.
Simon sat down a few feet from her. He was troubled.
He did not know how to dream.
Simon spoke softly,
"Shirley will you teach me how to dream?"
Shirley did not hear him. She was busy dreaming.
He asked again,
"Will you please teach me how to dream?"
This time she heard.
She turned to Simon
with fresh dreams in her eyes and smiled.
"Surely," she said.
"Relax," she continued, "there are no rules.
Think joyous thoughts. Let yourself be free."
After a few frustrating moments Simon spoke,
"I'm afraid I need some more help."
Shirley giggled.

"Okay, Simon Square, look up at the sky.
Imagine what it would taste like."
"Ummm . . ." Simon thought and imagined.
"It would taste like . . . a popsicle!"
They both smiled and imagined
licking the popsicle sky.
Then Shirley spoke,
"I imagine the sky is a great river.
I let its smooth current take me to strange lands . . .
and sometimes . . ." she continued to speak,
but Simon had stopped listening.
He was being taken away by the
sky's smooth, flowing river.
He was being taken to a land where
he was a knight with shiny armor and
rode on a black horse and carried a magical sword.
(Even squares have heard of magical swords.)
He was dreaming . . .
Soon Shirley was dreaming as well . . .
After a time they came out of their dreams.
Simon felt so relaxed and happy.
He told of his brave stallion named Rideron.
He told of castles, dungeons, goblins, and wizards.
Shirley told of rainbows, elves, pixies,
and lush green meadows.
"Shirley, you have shown me how good the earth feels
beneath my toes!
And Shirley, you have taught me
the magical gift of dreaming!
That is the most valuable lesson of all!
I thank you from the bottom of my heart!"
Then a sad thought came to him.
"You have taught me so much
and I have taught you nothing!"
"Simon, that is not true.
You have taught me the most valuable lesson
a dreamer needs to know.
You have taught me
there is a time and place for dreaming.

I thank you."
Simon, however, was still saddened.
Just then a flock of geese flew overhead.
"I wonder why they are flying in a V-shape?"
Shirley asked, not looking for an answer.
"They fly in a V-shape because it is easier that way.
One goose is in front.
He breaks the wind for the others.
It makes it easier for them to fly.
When he is tired he goes to the back of the 'V',"
he said in a flat tone.
"Oh, that sure is nice of them." Shirley replied.
Then Simon became excited.
"Shirley, I can teach you all the things that you may
have missed because you were busy dreaming!"
"Oh yes, Simon, that is a wonderful idea,"
said Shirley Circle.
So he told her that geese
have the same mate all their life.
"That's the way it should be," she replied.
And he told her all the names of the flowers.
"I've always loved them.
Now their beauty has a name!"
Shirley remarked how beautiful the sunset was.
Simon told her that the colors were so vivid
because of dust in the atmosphere.
She said the sun looked like a huge scoop
of orange sherbet that was slowly melting.
He saw the sherbet.
He saw the beauty.
She understood about the dust in the atmosphere.
She was glad for knowing about it.
It made the sherbet more beautiful somehow.
Then the stars poked through the night sky.
They looked like needles in a black pin-cushion.
Simon told Shirley that the stars were millions
of miles away.
She decided that she would visit a star someday.
Simon was about to tell her that was impossible,

but instead he asked if he could come along with her.
Her smile was answer enough.
The moon was full and bright.
Shirley Circle said she saw a face in the moon.
Simon Square told her of the meteorites
that had caused craters in the moon.
She was glad for that, she now knew the smiling
face on the moon was made by meteorites.
With the shiny stars millions of miles above,
and the meteor-made face of the moon
smiling over them, they were happy.
The happiest they had ever been.
And they didn't know why.
"You have taught me so much Simon Square.
I thank you with all my heart!" said Shirley.
"And you have taught me how to dream!
Oh thank you Shirley Circle."
They smiled. Then a moonbeam shone
directly upon Simon and a moonbeam shone
directly upon Shirley. They were both shocked!
"Oh my goodness Simon, are you sick?
You are purple! Where is your lovely blueness?"
"Look at you Shirley, you are purple too!
And you are not totally round anymore!"
"And you are not totally a square anymore!" she said.
"We seem to have lost our shapes and colors!" he said.
In spite of their lost identities they began to laugh.
They were so happy it did not matter
what shape or color they were.
They were so happy and they did not know why.
Then Simon gave Shirley a hug
and everything fell into place.
They now knew why they were so happy . . .
Everybody knows that red and blue
make purple.
But what everybody doesn't know is that
when a red circle shares itself
with a blue square, it results in . . .
a very happy purple heart.

TO: Bennington College

            Bennington, VT

Lesley,

I'm sorry I have not written much. It seems life gets so heavy and tiring that I forget to sit down and enjoy your companionship. Lesley, for the first time since you've been gone I feel very far away from you. A distance that saddens me deeply. I hate the miles which separate us. I hate the distance . . . . I know our love is magical and true — Yes Les, my love for you is so true, valid, alive. It's the doubt, the brief evil moments of doubt that I despise. They seem to catch me at the happiest, most vulnerable of times. Evil whispers telling me of separation and how long it will be until I can hold you, kiss you, see you, smell you again. I hate the whispers. But through the doubt your smile always shines. I see your smile and the terror passes. I've never looked at the separation as a trial, a test of our love, but tonight I realized it truly was. I also know it is a test that we can pass with flying colors. So Lesley, if you feel me holding your hand tighter than usual it's because I love you so much and not because I'm afraid our grip might slip.

All my love I give to you in an invisible jug of Southern Comfort. Store it inside your heart and drink freely from it. Become intoxicated with my love.

Hello, Lesley,

How are you? I'm in Golden, Colorado
The Coors Brewery is somewhere.
Well, it's right there.
The houses and cars, highways seem
foreign and evil. They gather at
the foot of the mountains waiting for the
steel of civilization to grow powerful
enough to someday overtake the
beauty.

They're tremendously overpowering
(the mountains). I feel . . .
I want to climb into the mountains.
Not to the summit, not to say
"I climbed a mountain; thus I conquered it."
No, I want to hear birds,
wrestling instead of cars, flying
by on the highway. I'd like
to climb half a mountain, just
so I could look up and still
see a majestic creation
towering above just out
of earshot of people/civilization
but I know, if I climbed only half
or even the entire thing, I
would look down and see
a damn Texaco sign.

Hello, Lesley —

I hope you are filled with happiness — I am. Your love touches me. I feel it every day. Every sound. You have touched a part of me the rest of the world does not see. Through smiles and love, your love, I have let myself be touched by another, and it feels incredible . . . beyond love. We have united spirits. Shared our individual beings . . . and yet, I smile. I see how hostile love can be through the vulnerability of sharing, but the more we share the closer our spirits combine. Times like these I wish I was a poet — because the words, the emotions, are nothing less than poetic. The words, however, are simply words.

I wish the words, my words, could be whispered into your ear.

I love you . . . not three words, rather an emotion that words can never capture. I find myself wanting to say more, but words seem to be impersonal and foreign.

I hope I've said enough. I hope you don't need words. I hope you're full.

I am full. Complete.

I stand beside you always. And I smile. Of course.

*W*ell, there was Friday night.
Friday day, however, was a bit more
sobering. Yeah, Lesley, had my last
chemo therapy on Friday. It seems that
should call for a celebration right? Well, I don't feel I am ready
to burst out the champagne. It doesn't seem like it's over. Well,
I guess it will never be over. It's strange . . . the fear will always
be there. I guess a good thing. Fear helps keep me in line and
shows me over and over not only how precious life is, but how
quickly it could be taken away from you. If life wasn't so heavy
at times, we'd probably float away. I'm sure happy to know,
hair will soon be upon my body. Maybe it will come back red,
you never know. Thank God. Thank God it is all over.
One year of my life. Thank you, Les, for your love. Much of
the reason for my recovery is because of your love. Thank you.

Kiss me you beautiful creature.

Few words makes for few lies

*S*chool is strange. It's like somebody told this great joke, but nobody understands it. That period of minutes of searching for the meaning after the punchline, that's what school's like. Everyone is walking around with that confused look trying to figure out this joke. Then when you graduate, somebody tells you that there was never any punchline, and you realize the only thing funny was that there was not a joke. By the time you figure out the joke, all that time has been wasted because you realize that the joke is that there is no joke. Do you understand? I don't either. I didn't express that too clearly. I'll try again later.

Oh well.

Dad had a cup
>It was old and yet
>the best cup anybody could ever have.
>It was older than Grandpa.
>But it was good old
>like Grandpa.
>It was not made of gold.
>But it was warm to hold.

Mom taught me to fish
>and to wish
>upon a shooting star.
>But she'd always say
>that it is better
>to pray and
>thank Jesus the Lord
>for today
>than to wish.
>Because wishes don't always
>come from God.
>Prayers of all sorts always do.

They taught me to listen to
>the crickets that
>rub their legs together
>in quite a beat.
>To sing lullabies to
>the little babies who cry
>in the night
>with their moms holding
>them tight.
>And how their song ends
>at any first light.

• • •

I wanted to stay up all
through the darkness
to listen to the sound.
But I soon found my
head resting on
Dad's shoulder.
Mom and Dad even listened when I
told him of the bad times
in my room.
I told them of the green hairy monsters and
my certain doom.
Their eyes opened wide
and I knew in them I could
confide.
I told them of the growls and moans
that keep me awake
with all the noise they make
robbing all quiet and silence.
Dad said
with eyes still wide in his head,
that as many things
pound in the night,
the angels of light have already
won the fight.
So the next time you hear
creatures growling they are
probably just mad
because of the fight they
just had where they lost.
So you can just sleep.

Upward, onward

Upward, Onward
If I were an eagle I
       wonder where I'd fly.
If I were a deer I
       wonder how far I could run
without getting tired.
If I were a horse I
       wonder if I'd let anyone
sit atop my back. I
       wonder if I were a snake
       if I would be poisonous.
I'm not an eagle, for I'm
       wingless, or a deer for
       I have no legs to carry me.
       No one sits upon my back and
       a snake will never bite me
       for I am a tree, with
       my roots securely holding
       me in place. I have
       but one place to travel.
Upward to the heavens.

Caring Mom

A scraped knee.
A good report card.
A newly discovered loose tooth.
All these things mom is the first to hear,
Because her love and endless knowledge
        are held so dear.
A little dent in the fender.
The school principal not calling
        just to say hello.
A "D" in gym.
These things don't go straight
        to Mom, because of doubt.
But in the end, she seems to
        always find out.
When all the yelling and
        screaming is through,
three words do more than any paddle could do,
"I love you."

Gifts from above

I t was Christmas time again. Christmas, bringing endless batches of cookies portraying smiling Santas and button-nosed snowmen that idly wait inside assorted Currier and Ives tins to have their powdered-sugared heads bitten off and washed down with thick, rich eggnog. Christmas time, bringing well-dressed presents reclining under a well-groomed tree. Presents, rendering their well-kept secrets before wide-eyed, beaming children who pile their cherished gifts in a well guarded corner. They wait until it's their turn once more to run to the tree and choose their next, beautifully wrapped package of love, always saving the biggest for last. Christmas time, bringing over-drawn checking accounts, candy canes and people searching for the perfect gift. A gift some find singing age-old hymns in a candle-lit sanctuary and others find in crowded shopping malls where a jolly Santa hears the selfish tales of eager, little children. Children wanting the days until Christmas to pass as fast as Santa's reindeer fly across the snow-filled sky. For Roger Angelo, however, this Christmas brought him only one thing, another round of drinks.

It was December twenty-fourth, the night before Christmas, and while children all over Chicago dreamt of dancing sugar plums, Roger was numbing his mind with unhappy spirits. He sat on a bar stool, his eyes staring deep into a vodka and tonic. Bill the bartender, the only other occupant in the dimly lit room, was standing under the numerous neon signs and countless bottles behind the bar doing the last of the dishes. "The Scurvy Dog Bar and Grill" was Roger's home away from home. His real home, his one-room apartment, would soon be taken from him. He was three months behind on his rent and had been fired from his job at the ad agency four months ago. "The creative genius who tries to find his ideas at the bottom of a bottle winds up with only one thing, an empty bottle," they told him.

Mrs. Blanch, the hideous landlord, with her cigarette in mouth, crude curlers in her hair and tattered robe and slippers, would probably be waiting to give him his Christmas present, an eviction notice. Christmas meant little to her, and for Roger it hadn't meant a whole lot in quite a while either. His Dad had died when Roger was sixteen and since then, since that night nine years ago, he really hadn't had a Christmas.

Christmas at the Angelo residence could hardly be called a Christmas by today's monetary standards, but the love made up for the lack of funds. Christmas, bringing a tree cut from the woods in the dead of night by a laid-off coal miner. He would drag it in three feet of snow for nearly a mile while an idle flatbed truck, which would have gladly carried the load, remained outside in the forbidding Appalachian winter wind, trying to withstand the unrelenting snow that tried so hard to cover the rusted hood. A dead battery, and no money to pay for it, forced it to an early death. Christmas brought a teary-eyed, humble father presenting handmade gifts to his only child. Roger was just as proud and elated at the rough wooden cars and ships he received as any other child with his own special gifts. His father did try very hard, probably as hard as any man could, to make his son happy. The crude works of art, with the love of his father and Roger's imagination, became the expensive "hot rods" in the showcase at Woolworth's.

Imagining was what he could do quite well; he could imagine his dead mother's warm lips kissing him good night when his stomach cried from hunger and when the winter wind visited the small house through the thin walls. He could imagine the mansion he and his father would reside in when he became rich. They would sit by a flaming fire and have his servants wait on them hand and foot. He could imagine his Dad seeing the best doctors in the world and they would rid him of his hideous cough that strangled the breath from him. He could not only imagine such things, but he could cover countless naked pages with great images. Images transformed from his mind to paper. He could draw. His father would always smile proudly at the pictures Roger would create. "Art," he called them.

One such time, just two days before Christmas, Roger showed him a picture he had drawn of him — with his tired eyes and pale, wrinkled face — sitting in his favorite chair with its frayed slipcover and stuffing coming out at the seams. A tired smile crossed his face, his eyes gleaming with a pool of tears as he said, "Son, you'll go far." Then a troubled look came over his face as he took Roger in his arms. That Christmas was the best and last Christmas Roger ever had.

On Christmas Eve, his father gave him, wrapped in newsprint and tied with an old frail shoestring, a complete set of watercolors and five paint brushes all enclosed in an aluminum container marked, "Artists' Best Friend." They weren't like the watercolors Roger had used in school, but real, professional watercolors with every color under the sun, even some he had never heard of. That, as Roger thought back now, was one of the happiest moments of his life. Roger found out years later his father bought the watercolors with the money set aside for medication. His father died four months later of black lung disease.

The bar door swung open, welcoming the fierce wind and whirling snowflakes, revealing a figure. The man stood in the doorway, his top hat pulled down, shading his eyes. A brown, wool scarf complementing a beige trench coat covered what remained of his face. The door shut behind him. He waited until Roger's tired eyes acknowledged his presence. Only then did he take his hat off and peel away his scarf, revealing a black man with short, tight curly hair and a smile that, combined with his white teeth, seemed to light up the room. "Merry Christmas," he shouted, bringing a smile to Bill the bartender's face and causing Roger to stare again into his drink. The man shook the snow from his shoes and took the barstool next to Roger.

"Watcha having?" Bill inquired, wiping his hands on his dirty apron.

"Hot chocolate, the hotter the better," he said, having the smile still on his face. Bill turned away, eager to please. Roger sat, his fingers tracing the rim of the empty glass.

Bill returned with the hot chocolate and placed it on a napkin before the man.

"Thanks."

"Thank you." Bill said and turned away, disappearing into the back room.

A strange silence filled the air. The man turned to Roger and all in the same motion placed his hand on Roger's shoulder and spoke, "Why so glum?"

Roger turned to answer, but when his eyes collided with the man's, all sense was lost. The man's eyes, an endless ocean of serene darkness, along with his hand gripping Roger's shoulder, sent an overwhelming sense of warmth and contentment through his entire body. All the color seemed to vanish from the room, leaving only the man's eyes and touch. Roger was rendered helpless, staring at the man in a dream-like state.

The man's face was completely expressionless as he spoke. His voice traveled, not to Roger's mind, but straight to his heart. "Roger, I've been sent in peace to send you a message, a message of hope." He paused. "God has blessed you with a great gift. The gift of art, and just as He gave the world his most precious gift on this very night, soon you shall present your wonderful gift unto the world."

The grip was released, and the smile returned to the man's face as he turned to leave. A numbing sense of reality, like waking up from a bad dream, returned to Roger. The bar door swung closed, exposing a man in a beige trench coat once more to the harsh, winter wind.

Roger's eyes remained fixed on the closed door. His mind was a blur. Thoughts raced through his mind like moths gathering around a light. Who was that. He knew my name. I'd never seen him before. Maybe it was the alcohol. The gift of art? Give the gift to the world? How? Why me, God? Maybe it was the alcohol.

He turned his eyes from the door to take a drink from his quivering glass when he saw it. Next to the hot chocolate, with its steam rising from the brown mug, lay a gift. A gift wrapped in newsprint, tied with an old, frail shoestring . . .

Somewhere outside the bar, a hearty "Merry Christmas!" could be heard bellowing through the empty city streets.

*H*ow ya' doin' journal? Me?
All right. I finished my story —
Gifts From Above today. It was due
last Tuesday. I was happy that it
was done, but it seems so flat and lifeless now that
I've been working with it so long. Mrs. Schulz liked it,
"Marvelous," was the word, but I know I can do better.
Maybe next time I'm going to send it to Mrs. Rebholz for a
X-mas present. I really want to talk with her again. She is
a great person.

Kelly, a great person, as well as my first true love, is
coming home for Christmas. She moved to Missouri last year.
She was my shoulder to lean on and cry on all last year.
It will be weird seeing her again. Christmas is here again
and it seems that the magic it once held is slowly slipping
away. Now it's one more stress factor, but the vacation will
be great.

Basketball is . . . shitty. I'm improving a lot, but
dread the two hours of torture every day after school.
There's so many things I would rather be doing, but the
camaraderie is great.

School is just a six-hour routine that seems fruitless as
well as endless. Oh well, vacation is right around the corner.

I hate to leave ya', but its late and I have to get some
rest for basketball. I used to never go to bed before 12:00,
but my body seems unfunctionable without my sleep, so I'd
better cruise.

Later —

The bell tolls

The Bell tolls.
Black hooded knights steal the
       body from earth . . .
Never satisfied with the flesh
       their claws rip apart, hoping
       to reach the heart, the soul.
White robed saints stand by.
Usually smiling, they wait.
A new brother may soon be
       initiated. His robe ready
       to be donned
Not long now.

Content saints edge nearer.
The knight's burning eyes fuel
       their greedy hands that
       now have ripped the rib cage
       open, exposing the purest truth.

An answer soon.

Both groups jockey for position.
Eyes fixed upon a purple heart.
No longer does it pump blood.
It has become its own judge
       worst enemy, or possibly
       a savior.

Years flow by.
       Experiences, past events making
       the purple changes from darkness
       to light.

                  •••

Hearts become purple, neutral. But
      now is a scoreboard, yet
      still neutral. The perfect judge.
      It beats no more.
      The tallies counted.
           Judgment.
           Answers.

The saints turn away.
Heads shaking, expressionless.

Eyes of fire broaden evil, hideous
      smiles.
A horrid stench follows.

Rotten fangs devour the
      darkness, receiving new
      powers and strength.

The bell tolls.
Darkness reigns supreme.
Next time . . .
      Always next time.

Well journal, it's been a long time . . . Christmas once more brought a new year.

The past is nothing but experiences to shape the present. But right now is happening as we speak so I'll fill ya' in about it. Today brought a good day. I played a whole basketball game. (We played a weak team so the coach played the second-stringers.) I did quite well — 9 points, 2 blocked shots, couple of rebounds — all for a losing cause.

Could you?

Could you live where the laughter is only about you?
Could you live with a mind that seems to work
     like a machine badly in need of oil?
Could you live without the fear you will die?

Love and stuff

Words just words,
Actions in what is love again.
And can you show, prove love
Two different minds, different
            beings.
Keeping love . . . Impossible.
Love is not a prison.
But how can love be confined in a
            simple cell?
Love must be completed in a circle
            or else love is lost.
Forced love is no love at all,
            just a constant struggle.
A smile is not everlasting
            or a kiss.
A lifetime never long enough for
            true love.
How? Why do we have
            a constant struggle.

The river is dry, waiting
        for rain to fall.
Waiting for the spell to
        break its illusion to be seen.
The phone lies idle; its tail
        coiled waiting to strike.
You're gone — or was it
        I that left.
No matter
        the rain shall fall from
        a sky of happiness
        one day soon.

Open doors, closed minds

I opened the doors again
        today.
I sang the hymns, prayed my
        prayers.
My eyes and ears were wide
        open, but my mind was
        astray.
I played my part in the performance.
I received
        no applause or curtain calls, just
        the sound of the doors closing
        behind me.

The eyes

Deep oceans of blue
      surrounding, trying to engulf
      a black, seemingly endless
      tunnel of unknown fear.
The blue, so very blue, So
      pure and gentle always
      entering the darkness.
The darkness greedily welcomes
      the lush blue, polluting
      the purity and eternally
      staining the blue.
But the unrelentless persistence
      of the blue carries it once
      more into the foreboding tunnel.

The whispers like a cold wind
> burn my ears.

Their pointing fingers are loaded
> guns firing invisible bullets
> through my being.

Their staring eyes, vast hollow
> holes of hatred.

Their giggles bring no joy.

I'm blank.
> Different.
> Difference in their eyes meaning
> weakness.

They've found power within their
> similarities.

I've found power in separation.

Their weakness, I've found strength.

False love, real consequences

I came to being through the love
That you two seemed to share.
A night of passion, unsure minds
and starry-eyed stares.
You played the games and rolled the dice
A little wine and beer.
They dulled your moral minds and
thoughts.
You had nothing to fear.
So, I was brought to this world
The love not there, just fun.
But I was happy never-the-less,
I would soon see the sun.
Her tearful nights that soon came.
They shook me, but the joy
Was still in my heart. I then knew
I was becoming a boy.
The fights soon followed tears and pain
all around I became afraid.
Me and her stomach growing fast.
I wish he could have stayed.
The trip to the clinic. I sensed
The certain hurt and doom.
She feels deep inside, I was scared
For my home would be a tomb.

The pen, unsheathed.
The paper, happily sacrifices
       itself.
The mind, searching.

Words find order, meaning.
The mind still searches.

Words are still words
emotionless and weak.
But the mind still searches
       hoping to find a way
       to give words a soul, never
       succeeding, just discovering
       new words.

And so it goes.

A solemn spark gone
seemingly unnoticed.
The mind feeds the hungry glare.
Muscles tense.
Words being idle.

Eyes of fire, burning sense
from the mind.
Acts and words are swift.
Thoughts come far too slowly.
Trouble multiplies rapidly.

Fire brings smoke
Clouding the eyes,
Bringing only tears.

Sole

Upon a mountain where no human
        sole has ever stepped.
There lies a flower.
A flower no human has
        ever seen.
A flower whose fragrance no human
has ever experienced.
Whose shape no geometry
        class has ever constructed.
And the moment the soul of a
        sole steps upon the mount, the
        flower, fragrance, and shape shall
        wilt and die, for the human
        shall give it a name, a word.
        It shall die from the name.
        Its personal noun
        shall not be descriptive or
        objective, but much
        rather its obituary notice,
        so let us never let a human sole
        walk upon the flowered mount.

Music is a poetry reading
        complemented by melody.

No dimmed lights or spotlights
No director shouting "Action!"
No opening curtains.
Plenty of actors, the stage — school.
Plenty of audience, little applause.
The production beginning with the
       resounding ringing of the
       school bell.
Everyone fell into place accepting
       their roles, whether they were the
       stars or simply extras.
Plenty of costumes to match the
       actors' roles.
No dialogue
Plenty of gossip
No strike or curtain calls
Plenty of cast calls
Only for the stars.
No written script
Plenty of improvisation.
No reviews
Plenty of criticisms.

Parents and other not-so-pleasant thoughts,

I'm gone to rehearsal. The long list has been eradicated.
(except Ruffer's cage)
Be back????? Never.

Love,
Spenser

I didn't know her,
       but her eyes told me her
       story. I had never seen such
       brilliant eyes, but now the sparkles,
       were drowned in forming tears.
I knew the story, the story
       more than one pretty face had told.
I realized that even though her beauty was great,
       I was in no mood
       to hear some girl tell me of her
       broken heart and lost love.
So instead of asking to buy her a
       drink, I finished mine and turned to
       leave.

Sage

So you're a big teenager, eh?
So you get to wear makeup.
     Wild clothes
     Talk back to
          your parents
     Right?
Wrong. It only means
   that you can mow
the lawn, feed the dog,
and take out the trash
without being asked.

Knowledge changes the state of mind, but emotions
       are an
       illogical form of knowledge we
       should never argue with.

I'm tired of finding nothing but
       air in my palms.
The meanness in people's eyes is hard to
       look at without sunglasses.
My Ray Bans I lost long ago.
They lie next to my crucifix and '54
       Topps Willy May's card.
The glasses sheltered my eyes.

Today, soon to be tomorrow. (A thoughtful collection of thoughts by Spenser Somers)

Alone again with my thoughts.
Good ol' Simon & Garfunkel
to keep me company.
I don't feel poetic or
creative, just confused.
A D+ in biology possibly.
An "F" in geometry.
A senior girl, not a girl,
a woman for a
girlfriend.
She's the most beautiful person
beautiful inside and out.
Well, this journal is going
to be awesome!
For writing is my love
as well as my hobby,
and some hot poetry
and intense stories are
going to give these naked
pages something frickin'
hot to wear!

So I am goin' to die, eh? A guide to the living

*S*o I am going to die, eh? Well then I must tell some tales so that when your time comes you will be ready. Am I ready? I don't know. I feel how warm my bed is, and how soft my faded Levis are, and how good my hot tea tastes right now and death seems far away. But it casts a shadow on me right now — as it does for all of us. My "shadow," however, has become more of an illumination than darkness. The light of death has taught me many things and I believe it is making my tea taste better right now.

My spirit has been lulled
        lately
By the sweet whispers of
Eternal rest. My eyes burn
with exhaustion. I sleep too much
but am never rested. Going up
stairs causes me to lose my breath
and every time I have
to go to the bathroom I sit
because I don't know if I could
stand up that long.
It has been a misty, tiring
        couple of days.
But in the midst of it all today
I could pray for the first
time. It was the strength
I needed and I rejoice for
the battle has already been
won. I am healed.
I am healed.
I call for health.
I call for healing.
Jesus has won.
By His stripes I am healed.

I'm trying to find God. Feel him
and receive his healing strength. I'm
on a quest of sorts. The journey has been long so far.
    A book? A story? These
are not the purpose of this
journey — books and stories have
endings and I fear I could not write
an ending.
1. Goodness
2. Love
3. God
    So it begins. I'm
    going to meditate.

Life is what you make it,
    with a little luck and a
    God that smiles upon you.

Life flows through the body like another
    drought coming to the mind.
    But the rain falls elsewhere.
    Great drought shall come, not
    to the body, but to the soul,
    And the soul shall evaporate continuing the
    cycle.

It's a matter of hours, a matter
of minutes transforming into
hours, where I once again embark
upon a journey. I'm going to
a land visited often. Children's
Hospital. A joyless place. White
sterile ghosts armed with steel needles
make for a haunting experience.
An experience I endure with my
eyes closed, my mind traveling
to peaceful lands inside a sleeping
subconscious. Five days. Five days
of constant nausea and dull pains. A
reality that must be endured.
The sun shines but cannot penetrate
a room when the shades are pulled.
Pain and nausea cannot be felt by
a numb mind. Reality must be
endured so the sun can be seen
and emotions felt after five days.

Soon be upon us.
The hair is falling out — shitty —
It's all starting to weigh heavy inside of me. Life's simplicity has gone away, it seems. I'm tired of thinking about things . . . I'm sad . . . sad, but not angry. I don't want to be angry . . . . I just want to be able to run. Let the speed of my legs lift me away . . . Yes, to run.
But, I have your hand and my faith to help me walk.

It's strange to think how good a random high-5 or hug can make a guy feel.

Thoughts of old thoughts of gold

No one knows the pain I've experienced
        the tension and emotions knotted
        so tight inside, strangling
        my heart.
Thoughts of happiness blurred
        by the nightmare of
        reality surrounds me.
White, sterile ghosts
        haunting my everyday life.
        For their years of schooling search
        a verdict.
A sentence of living hell.
Be strong and smile for hell
        cannot be reached without
        death, and death will never
        bring hell, but true happiness
        can only be found through death.
        And this I pray will be soon.
Happiness sooner than anyone reading
        this.

There is a time when we all look
back on our life and feel thankfulness or
resentment toward those who
shape our character.

December 29, 1989

My Dear Sister Sage,

    I don't really know why I'm writing this. I don't know what I want to say. But I do know there is a lot that needs to be talked about. I guess the first thing I'd like to say is that I love you. I wish I could take away all your hurt feelings with those three words, but I can't. Sage, I am very sorry that you feel neglected. I'm not going to argue with you about that, because that's how you feel. I know also that you have every right to feel hurt. I probably have been getting most of the attention lately. I'm sorry Sage that you feel hurt. But I can't make excuses for my sickness. I do need special attention sometimes. The doctors say I don't have much time to live. That means I may die soon. Sage, what I want you to understand is that it isn't fun "getting the attention." You talked last night about the family reunion. Well I gotta tell you it's not fun answering "How do you feel?" a thousand times. I get tired of being happy. I want to cry a lot (like right now). This cancer stuff is hard on all of us, Sage. Think how hard it is for Mom to be faced with the thought of losing her son. Sage, now you're probably feeling bad for "feeling bad." But, Sage, don't. It was good that you told us how you feel about things. It was good to get it out in the open. I'm just beginning to realize that my darling little sister is a young *beautiful* lady. You are to be admired, Sage. You have never complained about much of anything. You bring me happiness. I think a lot of happiness comes because you *don't* feel sorry for me. Sage, I can't tell you how much I appreciate that. I wish more people would treat me like you do — as a normal person.

    Love,
    Spenser

Personal Reflections

I almost tied my shoes today.
　　　　I almost set my alarm.
　　　　I just about turned my
　　　　　　stereo off.
I set my school books out
　　　　today. Their warm waters
　　　　of knowledge beckoned me
　　　　to dive in, but I thought
　　　　　　I'd drown.
　　　　I almost combed my hair
　　　　　　today.
Thoughts of mousse, hair spray,
　　　　and even new shampoo
　　　　　　entered my mind.
A tan might do me good as
　　　　　　well.
Some new clothes might bring
　　　　more telephone calls.
The mirror contemplated my
　　　　being for a long while
　　　　　　today.
Tying my shoes might cut
　　　　off the circulation.
Time will always be here,
　　　　and my stereo keeps me
　　　　　　company.

　　　　　　　•••

The waters inside books are
       nothing compared to the
       ocean around me that
       needs only to open my
       door to be discovered.
Combs, hair spray, mousse, tans
       and new clothes can never
       bring more telephone calls,
       only superficial conversation.
For nothing else matters as long
       as the man in the mirror smiles back
       at the lowly being standing before it.

He came to me young and strong, a boy
        who had so much to give.
His hair was blond, with laughing eyes
        the ultimate, yet to live.
His smile had rays of sunshine, warmth
        that shocked souls.
The friends were many, troubles few.
        He'd soon be paying the tolls.
He said he'd felt a lump inside
        his chest. He took some tests
I told him "Don't be scared." He tried
        to smile. He did his best.
The tests did confirm, fears lurked
        deep inside.
Shadows that consumed
        logic from his mind.
The years of school, a dream.
The walk to waiting rooms to tell
        that one more life may end.
The journey walking on knives.
I wish it was pretend.
The sentence — hell.
The boy's laughing eyes now are closed
        The struggle over.
The joy we will soon know has become his.
The dream of an innocent boy.

Death is so often paired with
       darkness for me; however it
       is the sun's bright illumination
       showing how wonderful life can be.
       Tomorrow a gift to be opened.
       Today's wrapping paper thrown
       aside, its secrets revealed.
       The gifts from God.

Blankets upon my residency, a bed, bring
       the warmth, once found inside a
       loving parent.
No milk feeds me, instead
       nutrients are absorbed from
       a needle, intravenously.
       Struggling for my first gasps of air so
       long ago brought life,
       separation from mom.
Now my gasps for the precious
       air shall soon bring me to her.
I shall see my mother soon.

Scars that smile

While the hideous cancer became obtuse with my very being.

While the constant pain in my mother's heart showed only in her scared hollow eyes and the long solemn hours of prayer.

While the powerful drugs made my hair flee from my body exposing a naked soul, a soul that for the first time had to be confronted.

While the pounds dropped and the muscles shrank, I became no more than a mind with a useless body.

But the mind accepted the body as well as the soul, and superficial became just a word.

The acceptance brought happiness and true love for the first time.

And through the strife and pain found my own world.

A world deep inside of my mind, a world lonely blank pieces of paper wanting only to take me away to undiscovered lands of smiles.

And at night coming out of my world with my mind racing and heart laboring, I would smile, for I knew that my world would always be here for me, beckoning me back into paradise.

When I was young, my
        mother tied my shoes.
When I was an infant
        I was barefoot.
Adolescence came and my hair
        kept my shoulders
        company.
I was born without the
        burden of growth upon
        my head.
Manhood brought the fierce
        cold-steel rungs of the
        corporate ladder.
        The warmth of a love
        who's gone.
Later my mind became immersed in the
        river of love only to
        have my heart swept by
        the currents downstream to
        the sea of despair.
Now white ghosts haunt
        me every day. They tie
        my shoes. I want to be barefoot.
        Hair has fled my head again.

I *have just come home from a five day*
hospital stay. Chemotherapy. As I said
earlier, pain has been with me for some
time. Pain, however, is not the word to
describe chemo. It is more a struggle. A struggle of a numb
mind fighting. Keep the body numb and reality is a blur.

I've tried to keep cancer from interfering with the rest
of my life, but the mirror's reflection tells a truth that can't be
argued with. Yes, I am bald, the hair on my head fled nearly
three months ago. But cancer hasn't stolen my smile and
never will.

Being bald is the second time shampoo and haircuts
have become pleasures for others who forsake the exercises.
When was the last time you thanked God for the simple
delight of having hair? Or for breathing? But as I was
saying, being bald was and is an experience that has shaped
my character. The first relapse was in ninth grade, a time
when you are struggling to find who or what you are and at
the same time trying to be like everyone else, a terrible time.
A time when insults upon others are your building blocks for
yourself. A time of cliques whose circles are so tight many get
strangled by them. But we all seem to survive the ordeal and
find that after the storm we all seem to wash up on our own
beach and find our private island Paradise in knowing our
true selves. Sure, few find the tranquility of the sun and the
sand in junior high, or high school, or even college. They are
the ones still lost in the immense ocean. The lost ones. But for
me, however, my storm brought no falling precipitation,
but falling hair.

Eternal venture

A wave of anxiety flows once again.
Senses sharp and alive, waiting, hoping.
   The end of the quest near at hand.
But the seemingly endless labyrinth wings on,
A moment of fulfillment followed by years of
   discouragement.
The brief moments of possible discovery beckon
   me only deeper into the maze.
   Some call me a fool,
   A blind man seeking sight.
But, I've chosen my own blessing, for some day
   complete fulfillment will be mine.

Death's song is heard daily
        I've turned my rock n' roll up louder,
Heaven's song accompanies the
        crickety rhythm and causes me
to "Now I lay me down to
        sleep.
I pray the Lord my soul
        to keep."
The doctor's words, my mother's tears.
I listen and it's played
over and over. I've tried to sing the
        hymns louder.
I'm alone and the chorus
        echoes through my
        body, taking energy for the sake of song.
I lay my body down to
        sleep. The song mellows.
The cricket is silent
The song is
        a pleasant lullaby
        for my soul to forever keep.

        Sorrow is so empty.
        Like eating only a salad (without dressing)
for dinner.
        Smiles fill the soul.
        Surely smiles (laughter for an appetizer), are
the meat and potatoes that make up the entree of
happiness.

I believe that when you die your spirit leaves the body and goes to heaven. The spirit/soul is the manna, or God inside us. Once we die our souls go to where the source of all manna/God/life is. If the goodness is manifested inside us.

I ran up the stairs today!
It feels great to be able to feel
God. To feel good, or rather to
feel God. That is great.

We laugh and cry,
      for soon we shall die.
Hatred burns, yet the heart
      still yearns for a place
      where we all will win the race.
      Where we all will smile
      And even talk for a while
      Expressing our true goodness.
      No more sin, no more distress
      Only a favorite story to confess.
Closed doors become open windows
Where is this place, no one knows.
Easier to laugh than to cry.
Clothes cover our evil flesh.
Curtaining doors to leave the world
      outside.
The mind imprisoned
      by a sinful being.

The wonderful irony of life (and death)

Isn't life funny.
Isn't death hilarious. It is for
me. See it has taken death
or the fear of death to finally
live. It doesn't matter if
I have tomorrow because I've
had today. That's living, man.
To finally trust God completely.
To praise God, to give thanks
to Jesus when you are stuck
in traffic with a headache. One of
the most powerful prayers we can
pray is "Thank you Lord God for
right now. Thank you for all the
events in my life that you
have brought to me right now. I
praise you for my life and all the
experiences that have brought me
here (in a car stuck in traffic, in
the living room watching TV, or
in a hospital bed about to die)."
To finally submit ourselves
to God and praise him no matter
what the situation is, that is
to have lived. To let God be God

...

and let you be you. That is
to have lived. To humble
ourselves long enough to admire the
vast power of creation. That is
to live. That is power. Once
you give your life away then
you finally have somebody. Once
you admit you are a fool
that is the first step toward
wisdom. Once you lose the
blindness of selfishness
that is the color of life.

> Life is funny.
> Death is hilarious.

ell, it's time. It's time to tell my story. I am driven to immortalize myself on paper. Driven, not because my life may end soon. No. I'm driven to tell of the new life I've discovered. The bright light of life I've found. The light that casts a large shadow, the ominous shadow of death. It takes light to cast a shadow, every positive accompanying a negative. The negative, the cancer inside of me. The positive, my spirit that grows along side the cancer. Which one, the cancer or spirit, shall become triumphant. Time and God only knows. Either way, I come out a winner.

I often wonder whether God is building my character for the future, or if he is simply making me an example to the rest of the world, on how to accept suffering. Either way I come out a winner. That is the way I concentrate upon the positive.

Death is like the sun. Its light showing how wonderful life should be. People die every day, their light extinguished; yet the sun still shines elsewhere. The sun is for the living, reminding us of the dead, and revealing all of life. The sun sets only to rise again.

The "sun of life" may soon set for me, but I have seen the love, beauty, and smiles the day has brought. I don't fear the dark, the night, because I've seen the light of day. Even though the sun of my life sets, it will rise again, as I will rise again to see the eternal light of love. And how gloriously bright and warm the light will be. God's loving light to keep my soul warm. We all must bathe in the light of life, for soon we will be swimming in the light of death — God Bless

In Memory

Spenser John Somers was born on February 21, 1972, in Kansas City, Missouri, the son of John and Karen Thiele Somers. On April 2, 1972, Spenser was baptized into Christ at Trinity Lutheran Church, Mission, Kansas. In 1984, Spenser moved to Edina, Minnesota with his family. They became members of Cross View Lutheran Church, Edina, where in 1986 Spenser publicly confirmed his faith in Jesus Christ.

Spens played basketball and baseball in grades 9 and 10 and was vice president of his junior class. He was on the staff and was published in Edina High School's literary magazine, *Images on the Wind*. He was selected to read his work at the Loft in Minneapolis. Spens was elected 1989 Homecoming King at Edina High. He graduated with the Class in 1990, being selected "most respected person" and receiving two standing ovations in response to his commencement ceremony speech.

Spens served two terms as vice president of Jubilee, the senior youth group at Cross View Lutheran Church. He was also an active member of the Oasis Senior Youth Group. He did volunteer work with Sister Jean's Mercy Missions Cookie Cart, a bakery in north Minneapolis.

Spens will be remembered and cherished for many things — his deep, personal commitment to Jesus Christ; the twinkle in his eyes that spoke of kindness and love; his dream of being a writer and the fine writing he left behind; his great love toward his parents and toward his brother, Sam, and sister, Sage; his courage in the face of chronic illness; his sense of humor, his creative spirit; his love of prayer and meditation; his wisdom beyond his years; the high value he placed on friendship; and the ability and privilege he had to touch many lives.

On Friday, November 9, 1990, Spens entered heaven after battling cancer and its side effects for five years. Spens is survived by his parents, John and Karen, a brother, Samuel; a sister, Sage; and grandparents, Elsa Thiele and Vern and Ruth Somers, all of Norton, Kansas. (Elsa Thiele passed away May 10, 1993; Vern Somers passed away June 19, 1993.)

Thanks be to God who gives us the victory through our Lord Jesus Christ!

Pallbearers:
Danny Arom
John Chapman
Christopher S. Davis
Miguel A. Fiol
Neil R. Johnson
Ryan S. Lund
C. Eugene Munster
Clark Schumacher
Kurt H. Vickman

Tunghai Da Xue
Taichung, Taiwan
Republic of China
November 10, 1989

Dear Spens,

Something about this culture is very relaxing, yet also very strange. It wraps itself around you like a warm blanket, or a Karen hug, and if you let it, it is very comforting and secure. Of course, to some this would be seen as a hindrance, an overprotective mother, but to me it is very fulfilling. It brings out the best in me by actually making me relax down to the core (soul). When I say relax, I mean relax. Sort of similar to the feeling you have after a rough massage; you don't want to move or do anything at all.

It's funny, but I know my relaxing, letting go of dreams, hopes, stress, $, etc. is what made me sick. I've always been so strong with my body, telling it not to be sick, not to be tired, hungry, even sexually motivated. I guess I would say I've been an intense person, you would call it a stressed person. But here I just am, the Sam that has always been there, the Sam that my friends during high school would say, "Are you O.K.? I've never seen you act this way. Maybe you shouldn't have that beer... ." I can actually enjoy doing things. Of course, they are things I want to do.

For example, I can sleep like a baby here. I'm talking deep sleep, almost dead, whoops just kidding. I've never been able to do that in my life. A pin drops and I'm wide awake worrying if we're lost or if my hair is parted on the side. O.K., yes, I did make that comment about the one-to-one relationship of hairstyle to career, but if you ever bring it up again I'll vehemently deny it.

Another not so good effect of Taiwan on me has to do with school, grades etc. Now I do things for myself, I learn for myself, and here's the hard part — on my own time schedule. It's like when Mom asked you to take out the trash right when you're in the middle of a ping pong game (me winning of course) and then an argument starts, when deep down you know you would have done it, eventually. No rush, especially for you. This is how it is with me now and school. I do the homework, memorize the characters, etc., but not because I want to get it done "on time" — which I usually do, but mostly just to enjoy the process of studying and learning. I've become a real student now and the problem is that now I want to follow my own mind, my own thoughts, not someone else's lectures, etc. I've rediscovered the joy of reading and the beauty of my own thoughts. Right now I'm like I was in my 4th grade class. I'd whip through all the "work" of the class so fast because it's so easy, just so I can read books, any books and think great thoughts. I guess what I'm saying is that I don't like *structure* anymore. I don't like teachers or classrooms or time schedules. I just like to sit, think, read and talk.

Do you hear it way over in Minnesota? Can you hear the Truth calling to you. Whispering to you in the darkness of night. Feel its breath gently caress your face.... It says:

"Don't worry, nothing really matters. The harder you try the more happiness will allude you. Sit down, have a glass of tea and all you really want will sneak up on you ever so quietly, steal into your heart, leaving you happy, satisfied, rich in spirit, healthy in body. But just try to turn your head and catch sight of those happy nymphs and angels and they are gone. Disappeared and won't return until you forget you were looking for them."

Spens, I love you. O.K., enough of that too, for when you talk of such things as love, like happiness, it too vanishes. You just have to come up on it from all sides, tease it to come out and show itself, to let the feeling be felt, not seen. This is how you write. You don't really say anything outright, don't shout that this is _____ (you fill in the blank: love, happiness, sadness). You just write with the feeling and it comes out in every word and phrase. Your writing has matured, but you know that every time you write something good. Oh yeah, disregard the other letter, for it was written before I received your "inspirational letter." I have complete faith in you now. That you can live if you want, or can do whatever you

choose. I hope you choose to dwell here on earth a bit longer.
(Read Richard Bach's *Jonathan Livingston Seagull* and *Illusions.*)

Now, how about a bit of Tang poetry before I go off for a nice nap . . .

In spring and autumn are many lovely day,
I climb a high place and write new poems.

Smiling on Jo-yeh Creek in spring

Seclusion on mind never ceasing,
From here I'll follow whatever I meet
Evening breezes blow my moving boat
on a path of flowers into the Creek mouth.
At night's edge I turn with the ravine
and gaze at the Southern dipper above the mountains.
Mist over pools billowing, rolling rises
a moon behind the forest.
Life's problems and deeds have swollen now to a flood,
My wish — to grow old fishing pole in hand.

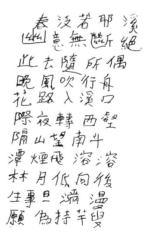

Hong Kong
January 1990

Dear Spens,

Well, bro, how are you? I mean how are you
really . . . I sensed something strange in my last call
home. I don't know exactly what it was but thinking
about, actually talking to Gretchen, an old friend from
Dartmouth, about it led me to come up with the cause
of your disease.

I call it the Jesus Christ syndrome. Billy Joel
knew it and sang about it in "Only the Good Die
Young." Being that (this) close to death really has
turned you into a great person. You are so happy,
so peaceful. You affect people in a good way, not me
of course, because I'm too stubborn to let my little bro
teach me anything. You have touched the world so
wonderfully, so why do I think that you are going to be
crucified just like the old J.C. before your ministry has
matured? Why can't you be like the Buddha who lived
for 80 years and taught the world so much? Why you?

On the phone you sounded so wise, yet I know I
can teach you a thing or two too. Oh Spens, I want to
come home now just to talk with you and teach you
what I've learned, loved, experienced here. You make
all the striving, studying . . . you make everything seem
so irrelevant. You bring it all into perspective, how yes
everyone dies, so live your life now, only now. Enjoy
every moment, be happy. Those are all Christmas
cliches, but they seem so true now.

God, this sounds like such a depressing letter.
I don't know if you understand what I'm saying, I hope
you're not offended at all. The basic point here is that I
love you and respect the way you've handled all this shit,
this cancer stuff. I still say you did it on purpose, so you
could skip school, sleep late, and wrap Mom and Dad

around your fingers. You sly devil, here I am telling you how great you are and what are you thinking, "but hah, if he only knew that this is the only way that I (meaning you) would get to live the perfect life."

Meanwhile you'd better be alive when I get home in February cause I really want to rap with you and to beat you up if necessary.

Your Brother

December 3, 1991

TO: Friends at St. John's University
FROM: The Somers Family
RE: *A Sense of Place: Saint John's of Collegeville* and
          a Sense of Peace for Spenser John Somers

A beautiful "sense of place" and sense of peace has come to me knowing that Spenser John Somers was a small part of SJU as a student for one week. The peace comes from knowing how he loved only a short week of classes there and the reasons he chose SJU for his college days. I can clearly in my mind see him walking down the walk on a lovely fall day, September 6, 1990 toward Tommy Hall. I waited for him in his room on 4th floor Tommy in the "L" of the building. He had stayed after to talk to Professor Boudreau, his Peace Studies Professor. I had come to pick him up from school to take him home for the weekend. Samuel, our eldest had returned from summer term at Dartmouth, and our family had planned to celebrate our 26th wedding anniversary together. I "see" him coming down the walk and my heart races to hug his lanky, tall, unconcerned how he dressed, body. He looked happy and well. I had worried and prayed for him all the week of September 2nd through the 6th as I knew, and so did he, that he was in kidney failure. His creatinine level was excessively high and that meant that he could go into seizures at any time because of the toxins in his body. Spens' friends cared for and watched him closely all that week, too. Spens knew he was being prayed for and loved there. The week was a good one. Spens and I talked on the way home about how he "related" to Professor Boudreau and about how much he liked him. He said how happy he was there and peaceful. Abbey Church gave him

solace and a time to pray and contemplate his future.
We talked about how beautiful the lake looked and that
I must bring a picnic when the leaves turned. He talked
about how wise had been his choice to come to SJU and
how perfectly right for him it had seemed over
Dartmouth, Macalester, Colorado College, or Carleton.

Spenser didn't return for classes at SJU, but he
remembered his time there with reverence and awe.
His health deteriorated from kidney failure to a
nephrostophy, to renal dialysis, to hospitalization.
A "Professor Tom Boudreau" continued to call
Spenser and our family and let us all know that the
people at SJU were all praying for him. Joel Kelly, OBS
Chaplain, came to Spens' Prayer Vigil on November 9,
1990 at our church, Cross View Lutheran in Edina,
to pray for Spens' heavenly reward. Jeanne Furst and
Tom Boudreau also came to pray. Joel Kelly also came
to Spens' bedside and prayed for him and for our
family, and thanked God for Spens' love for Jesus.
Joel was with Spenser at our home around 3:00 p.m.
Spens met his Father in Heaven that night at 6:20 p.m.
And all of you came to his "Homecoming Celebration"
on November 12, 1990 at St. Pat's Catholic Church.
You all touched our lives through Spenser and we will
always be grateful for the love and concern that you
felt for a young college student of only one week.
Thank you all.

John and I first met Tom Boudreau when he
came to our home the night of Spens' funeral. We had
spoken to him on the telephone several times after
Spens returned home from school. His soft-spoken
manner in explaining who he was and how much he
liked Spenser immediately caught my attention,
among the hundreds of well wishers, after Spenser's
Homecoming Celebration at our home. Here was a

person who had known Spens for only a few days and had in a short time realized Spens' creative spirit. Tom Boudreau is a quality professor, kind, sensitive and caring, a friend to the people in his classes. He apologized because he was meeting us at this time. We felt we already knew him by his caring, gentle spirit. Through talking with Tom, I learned that Spens had, in spite of his illness, continued to want to discuss the meaning of life with Tom and to continue to learn.

Tom telephoned later in the year to tell me that Spens' chair in Peace Studies Seminar was being left vacant for the entire year. The vacant place was to indicate Spens' presence rather than his absence. Tears of joy fell down my cheeks. Would any place, another school, or teacher, have done the same? . . . A "sense of place" and peace.

Tom called again later in the school term to tell us that at the end of the term in May, he would like the circle in his Peace Studies Seminar to be complete. He invited John, Sage and I to come and share Spens' writings with the class and to "fill in" Spens' place in the class circle. Tom also told us that one of his female students had returned from the Gulf War and if we could attend, the circle which had begun in September could "close" in May. On Thursday, May 17, 1991, we arrived and met in the Great Hall. Suddenly the warmth of the room and place seemed to envelope me and I felt peace and friendship and my grief seemed to lift in anticipation of sharing some of Spens' writings. Joel Kelly said the prayer in the classroom and we all joined hands. There we were where Spens had been and a place he had loved only a few months earlier. The joy and love felt that day and the sharing left by Tom will always be held close to my heart as it must have to Spenser. John read Spens' letter to his brother Sam about his philosophy of life, faith, humility and about his first bout with cancer. Sage read the "Flower Story." Friends of Spenser's, who also came to the class and viewed the funeral tape, read others. Then we listened as Joe Cavanaugh, an alumnus of SJU and special friend to Spens, related his love of Spenser's humor and wisdom from "The Walking Man" story, and quoted Spens' friend, Amy Clifford's poem she had given to Spenser.

> "A Spirit so powerful,
> it can breathe life into a
> pressed wildflower
> So bright, it can shed light
> into the deepest forest
> so soft, it can be a bed
> for a butterfly
> So peaceful, it can make
> the crickets stop their
> singing
> So loving, it can make
> my tears stop their
> falling
> This Spirit is SPENSER."

Then we viewed the video tape of Spenser's graduation . . . . He said among other words of advice, "I began to see that once you are at peace with God, peace with your fellow man comes, as well as, peace with yourself." After the readings, we shared treats and met the other class members. The love and peace of being in the circle where Spens once had been was certainly felt. Thank you Tom. After the class, Tom walked with John, Sage and me to Lake Sagatagan where we enjoyed the overwhelming beauty of a spring day and felt our souls touched by the peace and serenity of a "sense of place." The crew team was "putting in" the water. A 90 year-old Brother was fishing in his boat and gave the fish, I understand, to the monks at the monastery. I remember not sleeping well that night recalling Spenser and the day, but somehow feeling less grief, because we had shared part of his life at a place that had cared and continued to care for him.

The picnic lunch I had always wanted to take to Spenser came in the summer of 1991, August 22nd. Jeanne, Tom, my twin sister, Sharon, who was visiting us from St. Louis, and I gathered together for the summer-time picnic. We spread the quilt on the shore of the lake. We had tea, wine, barbecue chicken, fresh cantaloupe, potato salad and magic bars. We sat opposite the old, vacant chapel across the lake and the campus was quiet and peaceful. We felt Spenser's presence also! Jeanne and Tom spoke of Spens and how he touched them by his wisdom, humor, his writing, and his courage. Tom talked also about his time spent "sculling" on the lake and his love of SJU. In a time of fast-paced living, we four people had taken the time to enjoy a summer afternoon, shared a special place and a special boy. I remember thinking as we sat there by Lake Sagatagan that SJU is a very special place and God meant this to be a "little of heaven" on earth. My journal says at the end of the day, "I felt really peaceful and in touch with God sitting there with friends at the lake and I knew Spens would approve of our getting together there."

A year has passed since Spens attended SJU. We keep in close touch with SJU because his good friends, Kurt Vickman and Chris Davis, decided after going to Boca Raton and the University of New Hampshire, respectively for one year, to attend SJU.

They told me how beautiful the trees were this past
fall, and how much they knew Spens would have loved
to fish Lake Sagatagan and how they too love being at
SJU. Eric Soderlund, also a good friend and classmate
at SJU, wrote songs he played on the piano and guitar,
recorded the music, and dedicated the album, *Beyond
the Windows,* to Spenser. Danny Arom, too, must know
Spens is still there with him ... and others.

On Spenser's first anniversary into heaven,
Joel Kelly, OBS Chaplain sent a remembrance to our
family, that had been printed in your Campus Ministry
Newsletter,

"We remember Spenser.

We celebrate.

We believe.

— On Spenser's Anniversary —"

We thank you all for the love, comfort and a
"sense of place" and a sense of peace. You have given
much to our family and we'll always remember.

The Abbey Church calls me to come pray.
In quiet prayer and meditation, my life becomes more
harmonious and peaceful. I will come soon to SJU to
bring this note of thanks for a "sense of place" and a
sense of peace and feel the presence of God there and
in my life as well as "see" Spens walking happily at SJU.

Love,

Karen Somers

Spenser John Somers

(written by John and Karen Somers in February, 1990,
for Spenser's college application)

"Each one of us who travels further than the obstacles will know a different kind of life from that time on . . . ." (A Chinese saying) Spenser J. Somers has felt obstacles in his life the past four and a half years as a cancer patient. It is now mid-February and the coldness of a Minnesota winter has been warmed once again because he had great news after a chest x-ray showed no signs of tumors in his lungs. After six weeks of radiation therapy we celebrated! His gait is once again lighter, his brown sparking eyes twinkle, his smile is more radiant, his humor more profuse, and the love he radiates more vibrant. During days of chemotherapy, surgeries, CT scans, etc., he has never lost through these obstacles his special personality traits.

Spenser has always chosen not to let the obstacles of his illness interfere in his life more than the needed time for rest, recovery, and healing. He also has never allowed his family and friends to over-protect him, feel sorry for him or treat him "differently." Therefore, life has gone on as "regular" as possible for him because he is the one who never complains or feels sorry for himself.

The one quality that we see as his parents, that has built his character and made him the truly mature, likeable, lovable individual he is, is his faith in Jesus Christ. Joyful living is not an obstacle when Spenser knows that whatever road Jesus chooses for him everything and place will be great. His choice for a birthday and early graduation gift is to go for a visit to parts of Europe and on a pilgrimage to Medjugorje, Yugoslavia, where 15 million pilgrims from around the world have come to pray since 1981 and receive personal inner peace.

I have always loved him because of his great qualities of sensitivity to others and his humor. He has always cared and been concerned and helped the less fortunate. When he was little, he cared for the ring-necked snakes, the fish, and the animals. When I helped, through the Junior League, children of abusive parents, he was the one always who asked, "Why?" and "What can I do?" His eyes twinkle and little children are drawn to him like the Pied Piper. He has always given his love and attention to his younger sister and been sensitive to her needs, as well as those of his older brother. He planted wild flower seeds this past spring in a favorite "spot" for his girlfriend to share the blooms when she came home from college for the summer. He likes being with his family and we love that aspect of his sharing qualities.

His humor plays a big part in his daily make-up. He is fun to be around and funny. His life has had serious obstacles and decisions, but Spenser is able to see also the humor in most situations. We were driving back home after radiation a few weeks ago and as we paralleled a busy traffic street along I-35, I said, "Spens, I wonder how it would be to live here with all the fumes of gasoline?" He replied, "Exhausting!"

Spenser's quality of thinking and living life is mature beyond his teenage years. He has used his gifts, especially of writing, to turn the obstacles of ill-health at times into joyous times. Every day is good because he smells the flowers, hears the sounds of joy around him, and feels the goodness of life. To know him is to truly love him. We love him. He knows a different but good kind of life.

A "Memorial Series for Writers" at Edina High School, Edina, Minnesota has been established in Spenser's memory by John, Karen, Samuel and Sage Somers. The annual series has had the following guest authors:

Judith Guest
Roberta Whiteman
Lynne Westphal
Dr. Lon Otto
Jonis Agee
Michael Dennis Browne
Roseann Lloyd

The flower story

There came a time when the flowers needed to receive their scents. All the flowers were asked by Jesus what they wanted to smell like and whatever smell they asked, they received.

Now all the flowers were gathered in a lush meadow in heaven. All the angels were flying joyfully through the meadow, smelling the incredibly beautiful fragrances.

Finally, Jesus came to the last flower and asked, "What smell shall you smell like?" The flower was deeply frustrated and sad, but it finally smiled, saying, "Dear Jesus, I smell how powerfully delicious all these flowers smell. And I also have smelled the rain after it has fallen in the meadow. Likewise, I have also smelled orange blossoms. There are so many beautiful fragrances, dear Lord, I humbly ask that when people stop and lean over to smell me they will smell all the wondrous smells of the earth. That, Jesus, is what I ask."

Upon hearing the little flower, Jesus began to cry.

"My precious flower, you have given me more joy than all the other flowers. I will gladly grant you your humble wish. Because you have given of yourself so, I will give 100 fold in return. I shall make your petals yellow, like the sun, and as many petals as you have so many descendants shall you have.

"But, oh, little flower, I know people's hurts. The wind will not understand your precious humble gift. The world lacks humility. They will celebrate and cherish all the other flowers and treat you as a weed. For they know not the beauty of humility. So, my precious flower, I will give you a deep root. It shall cling tight and deep to the earth. As for your stem,

I shall make it so that the wind will blow and shall never break you."

And so all the flowers received what they had asked for.

And then all the angels blew a gust of wind and the flowers dropped to Earth. Adam and Eve smelled all the flowers and named them. They named Jesus' favorite flower "Dandelion."

(Cancer has taught me how to smell the flowers.)
Spenser Somers
September 1990

A Prayer Chapel dedicated to Spenser's memory has stained glass windows designed from "The Flower Story," the last story Spenser wrote. The Chapel windows, as well as the Chapel furnishings, were designed by Terry Helland, architect. Dick Rostal, stain-glass artist, made the windows. The Chapel is at Cross View Lutheran Church, 6645 McCauley Trail, Edina, Minnesota. The calligraphy for "The Flower Story" was done by artist Judy Dodds and hangs in the Prayer Chapel.